Axis of Evil
Understanding International Terrorism

© 2002 by George Yool

Updates © 2014

ISBN-13: 978-1500190699
ISBN-10: 1500190691

Contents

Introduction

> I resolve to speak ill of no man whatever, not even in a matter of truth; but rather by some means excuse the faults I hear charged upon others, and proper occasions speak all the good I know of everybody.
>
> —Benjamin Franklin

In these pages you will learn the true irony of the title, "The Axis of Evil," which is coined from George W. Bush's first inaugural address. I seek here to expose the true nature of international terrorism, explaining what it is, how and why it came about, and how it can be resolved. I will outline the greatest atrocities based on their impact with lesser sources of international terrorism. It is not my purpose to be an apologist, or an accuser. The purpose here is to overcome a very serious social problem that affects the safety and well-being of people around the world.

The reader will be shocked and dismayed at what they read in these pages. I cannot deny this. Although it appears that I do much finger pointing, my only reason is to expose the sources of terrorism for the purpose of resolving the problem before it becomes the trademark of the Twenty-first Century. In other words, this is intended to be constructive criticism. Therefore, my finger pointing shall be accompanied by solutions to the problems.

I begin my history in 1945, not because that is when international terrorism began, but because this is when modern international terrorism began. I am classifying it as modern international terrorism because of two factors: purpose and method. It should be noted that the countries involved have practiced forms of terrorism and international terrorism much longer. Starting in 1945, however, international terrorism spread like wildfire throughout the world on a grand scale incomparable with earlier atrocities. Many of the strategies for modern international terrorism were learned from the atrocities of Nazi Germany and the Empire of Japan, adapted, and then fine-tuned.

The terrorism of the late Twentieth Century basically fulfilled the prophetic view of George Orwell's book 1984. The world saw a perpetual war for power and resources waged between the North Atlantic Treaty Organization, Soviet Bloc, and China respectively. This drew the heat of the Third World War from the territories of the superpowers and put the battlefields in the Third World. The dismantling of the Soviet Bloc and USSR did not end the struggles in the Third World that had been staged by the First World. Now the Third World is struggling for its own identity and control of its resources, striking back at its former allies with the weapons it was given: namely modern terrorism.

Terrorism is no longer just an international matter, as domestic terrorism has also evolved to fight against the injustices of misdistribution or resources, wealth, and power. The real strength of terrorism is in religious fundamentalism not limited to Islam. It has reared its ugly head among Jews, atheists, Christian sects, Buddhists; really everywhere where subcultures are pushed to the brink of desperation. The fundamentalism evolves as a reaction to despotism, the lowest state of morality. At the roots of every terrorist group is a struggle for power against otherwise insurmountable forces. This form of war has raised its head every time a society has reached the peak of its power, when the people are most oppressed. The more arrogant and insurmountable the society, the more it oppresses not only its own population but any population it can drain of resources. It is because of this that the United States is the main real focus of terrorism around the world.

Terrorism is the ultimate state of guerilla warfare. It is the only way the civilian population has to fight against governments whose wealth and technology make direct confrontation impossible, and confrontation impersonal. Terrorism doesn't seek to win battles. Losing is actually the winning strategy of terrorism. Direct military action against terrorism actually fuels it. Terrorists are civilians striking against civilians and any infrastructure they can to disrupt the morale and power of the social structure they are fighting. We will explore the real sources and causes of terrorism, and ways to resolve it in this book.

Terrorism Defined

Introduction

While this book focuses on international terrorism, terrorism in general needs definition. Without local terrorist acts, there is no international terrorism. Therefore we must examine the critical qualities of terrorism.

What Is Terrorism

According to the USC Congressional and Administrative News, 98th Congress, Second Session, 1984, Oct. 19, volume 2; par. 3077, 98 STAT. 2707 [West Publishing Co., 1984]:

[An] act of terrorism, means any activity that

(A) Involves a violent act or an act dangerous to human life that is a violation of the criminal laws of the United States or any State, or that would be a criminal violation if committed within the jurisdiction of the United States or any State; and

(B) Appears to be intended
  i.   To intimidate or coerce a civilian population;
  ii. To influence the policy of a government by intimidation or coercion; or
  iii. To affect the conduct of a government by assassination or kidnapping

(Cited by Chomsky, 2001, p. 16).

This definition is notably ambiguous, with words like "appears to be" and "violation of the criminal laws." By this definition, a huge amount of simple domestic crime, especially everything covered by the Rico Act, or the Taft-Hartley Act (which was used against unions), would necessarily be classified as terrorism. For that matter, many campus demonstrations would also be terrorist acts.

Terrorism Defined

The Immigration and Nationalization Act is more explicit (Section 12 (a)(3)(B), specifying the following activities: hijacking or sabotage of any conveyance (vehicle); seizing or detaining, and threatening to kill, injure, or continue to detain another individual in order to compel a third person to do or abstain from doing any act as an explicit or implicit condition for the release of the individual seized or detained; a violent attack upon an internationally protected person (ref. 1116(b)(4)) or upon the liberty of such a person; an assassination; the use of any: biological agent, chemical agent, or nuclear weapon or device, or explosive or firearm (other than personal monetary gain), with intent to endanger, directly or indirectly, the safety of one or more individuals or to cause substantial damage to property; a threat, attempt, or conspiracy to do any of the foregoing. The act continues to identify actions deemed as "engaging in terrorist activity," ranging from preparation and planning to soliciting funds and membership (Chomsky, 2001).

The problem with the Immigration and Nationalization Act is that it is too specific in some respects, and simultaneously too vague. Again, because of its ambiguity, many simple domestic crimes would have to be categorized as terrorism, though they definitely are not.

Though everybody thinks they know what terrorism is, it is obviously an enormous ambiguity. We assume that every terrorist act involves some terrorist organization. The same position applied to everyday crimes would hold traffic violators as members of some gang or mob. Little do we realize that many lesser terrorist activity occurs independent of formal terrorist organizations. Typically, acts of terrorism do involve multiple parties, or conspirators, even if those conspirators merely supply the means (weapons) for the act. As a consequence, we cannot expect an act of terrorism to always be followed by an admission of responsibility by some terrorist organization.

The problem is to distinguish between a common criminal and a terrorist. To resolve this dilemma, we shall note that terrorism always has the following elements:

1. A crime or attempted crime committed for the purpose of
2. Attracting publicity that
3. Instills fear in the public for
4. The explicit purpose of
5. Causing an action or inspiring an ideological change
6. And thereby encourage the proselytizing of their own ideology

The sniper killings across the US in 2002 certainly put terror in the minds of many people, most notably in the Washington D.C. area. Americans across the country tuned in to the latest report on their local radio and television stations each day. This was not an act of terrorism because it lacked elements 4 thru 6 above. The Oklahoma City bombing also looked remarkably like terrorism. It, however, lacked the fourth element above, making it strictly an act of rebellion. One does not, however, need to capture the attention of international media, or even the media, to disseminate the fifth element, as the fourth element implies. In fact, it could be one of many events, a series of events, like guerilla raids, bombing by aircraft, etc. This brings us to the next phase of our definition.

Crimes Against Humanity

Now that we have some criteria, we can start dissecting the criteria for clarity. What, for example, constitutes a crime? According to the USC already quoted, this is based on State and Federal laws defining specific crimes. While that is okay to a point, it is negligent of the most serious crimes of all, which do not appear in either State or Federal law, namely crimes against humanity. For these I need to make a detailed list, as I seriously doubt one actually exists. Let us say a crime against humanity shall occur when a person, legal entity (e.g. a corporation), group,

3

organization, or government engages in, attempts to engage, aids or abets in the engagement or attempted engagement in any of the following:

- Genocide—The violent destruction of an entire race, religious or political group, class of people, or other category of persons within a geographically definable area

- Unlawful War—Since World War II, the old idea of warfare was supplanted with an ethical ruling that the only justifiable combat is defense. This has been twisted to include preventive preemptive strikes. The problem with preemptive strike is that all other measures must be exhausted first and the target of the assault must have the capacity, availability of resources, and propensity (criminal intent) to commit an atrocity a crime against humanity.

- Unjustified Violent or Coerced Overthrow of a Nation—What justifies the violent or coerced overthrow of a government is if that action is also a lawful war. If the intent, however, is to replace one oppressive regime with another, then there is no justification. No nation or group of nations less than the collective United Nations is justified in interfering in any capacity with another nation's government.

- Punishment of a Nation—The punishment of a nation in any manner, particularly the civilian population, is never justified. If the Treaty of Versailles and the consequent rise of Nazi Germany do not prove this point, nothing does. The people of a nation cannot be held responsible for the behavior of their government, even if that government acted as the people desired. This is not to say, however, that collateral damage of civilian assets is inexcusable, but certainly intentional collateral damage is an atrocity.

- Mass Simultaneous Violence—This is an extremely vague area, wherein murder, maiming, kidnapping, etc. occur. The term "mass" alone is ambiguous. Clearly the murder of one individual is as much a crime against humanity as the killing of a million, though on a much lesser scale. Typically, individual murders, even serial murders, are marked by a reason and a typology of victim, even if that typology is convenient (as with the Sniper killings). Mass simultaneous violence requires a group whose membership occurs at the same time and is based solely on where they are. It is also purposive toward an ideological end.

- Hate Crime—Another ambiguous term, applied to acts committed against persons based entirely on their membership in a particular group, but otherwise as impersonal as mass simultaneous violence.

- Assassination—The assassination of a political or religious leader is a crime universally agreed upon. It is a clear violation of the right of people to choose their leadership and to be exposed to a variety of different points of view. Assassination, however, must not be confused with the deposing legally of a leader, and later trial and punishment (including execution) of that leader for crimes they committed, as these are clearly the choice of the people.

Propaganda

The Twentieth Century saw technology change the face of war in horrible ways. Technology not only made killing more efficient, it made killing more accessible to both the perpetrators and the common person around the world. Prior to the telegraph in the Nineteenth Century, news could take days, weeks, even months to reach audiences. By the time news arrived, it was too little, too late. Even the telegraph was relatively limited. The radio and telephone gave audiences the opportunity to hear first hand accounts. Newsreels brought visual accounts within days or weeks. Technology brought conflict into the proximity of people far removed from it, and they were shocked.

Propaganda came long before these technological innovations. The technology, however, necessitated and then offered a means for disseminating propaganda. The necessity was in guiding the public toward the objectives of those in or seeking power. The Nazis and imperial

Terrorism Defined

Japanese were acutely aware of this necessity and explored the technology to mobilize their people. The Nazis really perfected this into a virtual art form.

The television took the American population by storm through the 1950s. When Kennedy was shot, Americans were watching. Their reaction to this and the "living room war" (Vietnam) showed the new current in public opinion. Johnson seemed unclear what to do with this social tool, while Nixon clearly mastered it. The reaction of the terrorist community was based on scale.

Large-scale terrorism, as we have seen in the methods, has a complex array of messages with at least three distinct audiences. The first is always a local audience, who must be terrified enough to not oppose the perpetrators openly. The second audience is the international political community. For this second audience the message is typically compliance: don't misbehave or you will be the next target. The third audience consists of allies and the citizens of the US and its allies. Here the message must be distorted and somehow justified, thereby assuring US and allied supremacy and affirming the power of leaders. Because of this, enemies grow stronger, and our civilians have the mistaken perception that our leadership is competently doing a good job to protect us from evil.

Small-scale terrorism does not have the same luxury of media control as large-scale terrorism. Their messages must then be more generic, and their purposes can be extremely ambiguous, as with the case of 9/11. On a small scale, as with much terrorist activity in Israel against the Jews, the message is directed at the local community and not so much the international community, and is typically an act of desperation (strapping explosives to your body and going into a bar is on par with the Oklahoma City bombing). The media, loving the sight of blood, cannot resist these, and is quick to show these people as radicals without delving into the causes driving the desperation.

On a slightly larger scale, terrorist groups will stage larger assaults that appear nearly random, such as 9/11 specifically to get the attention of the international community. Where a bomber on the streets of Israel is targeting whom he or she perceives as enemies, the terrorist groups are seeking to increase membership, promote the extent of their own power, and/or encourage the destruction of governments. This, in fact, appears to be the set of reasons behind 9/11. The show of power alone is great for recruiting a larger membership for the group's cause. When the act is reacted to with violence, the collateral damage automatically increases the number of sympathizers. As such, al-Qaeda succeeded in making Afghanistan a victim of US aggression, thereby strengthening Islamic resolve of the US being anti-Moslem, whether the assertion is true or not. Also, al-Qaeda is clearly against several Middle Eastern governments viewed as soft on the US. Because these governments supported the US assault, this increases social discord within those nations toward their own governments and the US.

Ultimately, the target of 9/11 was not the US. The US was merely an instrument to further the overthrow of local governments. They knew the US would not rest after such an assault, and that the US would react drastically and violently. They also knew that governments throughout the region would support the reaction in spite of local dissent, thereby sowing the seeds of greater discord. The US and Britain, foolishly, played along and acted nearly unilaterally. Had the US and Britain not acted unilaterally, but had sought solutions through the UN, this would have been counterproductive to the al-Qaeda objective. Basically they played the US like a musical instrument with great success.

Without propaganda, terrorists cannot fulfill items 4 thru 7 of our elements of terrorism. Terrorists are enabled to deliver their messages by the media's hunger for hot stories. Governments can then use the actions as propaganda for large-scale terrorism.

Terrorism Defined

The Nature of Evil

In literature we are often misled to believe that evil has a face. When an terrorist atrocity occurs, the faces of the terrorists and their leaders are displayed so we can see who it is we should be mad at. These are the so-called faces of evil. As we are to see through this book, the face of evil is not so easily shown. In fact, evil is more often faceless and the result of bureaucracy and common behaviors than we expect. Philosophers have argued over whether people are born inherently evil or inherently good. I tend to disagree with the assertions of both perspectives. Humans are born with the capacity to do either, and are often not conscious of acts of evil. Here our concern is not with basic evil. Basic evil is a moral issue of right and wrong. The concern here is with ethical misbehavior, which is far-reaching and typically faceless. Morality is what binds a society together, where the ethical makes us human. Few individuals in history have achieved a level of ethical evil worth mentioning. These individuals have the following traits: they exploit opportunities leading to personal gain, typically in the form of power.

Terrorism is a symptom, it is not the actual problem. The common person has little to no capacity for evil. They are easily malleable and led by basic desires for survival of themselves and the species. They are little more than animals in many respects. I know this sounds degrading to the majority of humanity, but let's face the reality, at least 85% of the population is completely subject to the conditions of their environment, which is typically dominated by the availability of resources, which are always minimal for the common person. The ranks of the common terrorist, the person who sacrifices himself for the sake of his cause, is not innately evil, no matter how despicable or atrocious the act he commits. He is merely a pawn, just like any soldier.

As I write, highly civilized human beings are flying overhead trying to kill me.

They do not feel enmity against me...nor I against them.... Most of them, I have no doubt, are kind-hearted law-abiding men who would never dream of committing murder in private life. On the other hand, if one of them succeeds in blowing me to pieces with a well-placed bomb, he will never sleep any the worse for it. He is serving his country, which has the power to absolve him from evil.

Orwell, "England Your England," p. 252 of A Collection of Essays

Orwell's statement combined with ultimate desperation and available opportunities are the earth and fertilizer in which the weeds of terrorism grow. When I consider Gaza Strip today, being blocked off with 100,000 families receiving basically flour and oil rations to live on from charities (whose money has run out), I cannot help recall the Warsaw Ghetto under the Nazis. The poor occupants of Warsaw's Ghetto were worse off, but not by much. They had no opportunity (e.g. weapons and leadership), and when they rebelled, the uprising lasted a month before the Nazis burned every block, killing or sending them to concentration camps to die. Gaza is millimeters from the same treatment at the hands of Israel. The irony is astounding, but not altogether surprising. After all, the conflict makes the Israeli government stronger.

Let us examine the position that the terrorist is merely a symptom, merely a common person led to an atrocious end. In common law, burglary required "breaking", which came to be interpreted as doing anything that would constitute entry into a contained space, like a home, including simply pushing open an already opened door (current law reads: entering and remaining unlawfully with the intent to commit a theft or felony therein— sorry, my legal training is showing through). It did not matter how the door was pushed open, whether an instrument was used, an animal, or even a child. In the end, the burglar who caused that door to open, that penetration of a closed space to occur, was guilty of the breaking. The device, animal, or child became an instrument of that end and was not itself guilty of the crime committed. Terrorists either live in or become sympathetic toward a social environment of destitution and oppression. One hears, for example, that one man's terrorist is another man's freedom fighter. This freedom fighter is a form of soldier. In the passage from Orwell, he observes that the Nazi bombers were law-abiding citizens, no more likely in regular life to kill a fellow human than anyone else.

What then drives this radical, fanatical approach of the terrorist? If the terrorist is merely an instrument of terror, then who is the actual perpetrator? We can try to point our finger at the leadership of terrorists, and find what we perceive as a level of evil, but this too is an illusion. The leadership of terrorists is dependent on opportunity. The opportunity is created by the oppression of an outside force, a force which creates the destitution that would lead any civilized being to uncivilized behaviors. It is nice to say you would never steal, but if your child was starving and you had the opportunity to steal and feed that child, you would. It is only natural. The Treaty of Versailles, for example, in punishing Germany created the opportunity for Hitler's rise to power. While it is understandable why the European allies insisted on the punitive measures, at the same time they inadvertently perpetrated an evil on a much grander scale, which could have been avoided given a little insight and a lot less emotional attachment (passion) to the pains of the war. President Wilson saw it, but was ignored.

The true source of the evil is the opportunity creator. This is not to say, as in the case of a burglary that merely leaving the opportunity available makes you both the perpetrator and the victim. On the contrary, the opportunity must be created purposefully as a means to a particular end. In the example of the Treaty of Versailles, the evil act in that case becomes one of negligence by this argument, because there was no mal-intent toward creating the new situation, merely neglect at observing potential outcomes. Why would someone want to encourage terrorism? The answers are too simple to imagine, and as the argument of this book proceeds they will become obvious. The first, and most obvious, is war objectives. In 1963, for example, the Department of Defense (DOD) presented a plan to inspire Cuban terrorism on US citizens. The purpose was to inspire public opinion to support an invasion of Cuba. JFK rejected the proposal. It is not clear why he rejected this proposal. For all we know, his attention was at the moment too focused on China's developments in nuclear weapons to worry about Cuba anymore, especially with the two failures he already had with Cuba (the Bay of Pigs in 1961 and the near invasion of 1962 which resulted in the Cuban Missile Crisis).

The other reason an opportunity will be created is even more sinister than the first, yet also related. The DOD in the former example wanted to be empowered by the population to act aggressively. Further back in history we can see both world wars were stories of opportunity. The assassination of Arch Duke Ferdinand allowed for an opportunity. Hitler made the Treaty of Versailles, which resulted in desperation in Germany, an opportunity to exploit. In both instances, leaders took advantage of a situation to create new opportunities for the fulfillment of their own power. The key to this is the ultimate reason for creating opportunities for terrorism: power. Terrorism creates fear, and fear automatically gives power to whoever the population feels will make them feel safe. The terrorists are the first line of victims of those who gain power by the acts of the terrorists. Like good mobsters, governments since World War II, fearing total nuclear annihilation, cannot risk getting their hands dirty committing atrocities personally. Terrorists, like drug mules, are the stooges and fall guys of those they are trying to attack. They are literally feeding into the problem they are combating.

It is a common problem in modern society to treat symptoms rather than eradicating the real cause of the ailment. Medical doctors struggle with this every day. Doctors know it is easier to treat symptoms in a reactive way, and much more difficult to observe the root causes. The reason is relatively simple: you don't realize you are on the path to the symptoms until you get there. The bad part is that treating symptoms often results in equally, if not greater, symptoms. In terms of social problems, and terrorism is a social, not a criminal problem, we often find that the source of the problem is something apparently innocent and innocuous; so innocent and innocuous, that we do not realize that we are the real source of the problem. American society, for example, is responsible for most of the pollution and waste in the world. Our consumer-driven society is completely unconscious of the harm it brings on the rest of the world, and worse, we don't care. In 1984, Orwell's hell is one where industry and science are geared toward war making. A society that focuses on war making is wasting resources that could better the markets it wants to exploit. War necessarily deprives people of resources, and it is in the deprivation where desperation arises, and from the desperation comes radical responses and ultimately power.

Given the history we will later discuss on the Middle East, is it really that surprising that these people who have nothing to lose would turn to blowing themselves up? Is it a surprise that killing a cruel jailor is seen as immediate passage to heaven? Combatants in these situations seldom bother to put themselves into the shoes of the other side. Every day I hear reports of Israeli troops killing eight, a dozen people, or more of all ages. Are they truly so blind that they cannot see themselves as perpetrators? They are quick to cite themselves as victims, but their families are caged not by walls, barbed wire and guns (as the Jews in the Warsaw Ghetto were, or the Palestinians in Gaza today), but by their own fears. They are quick to call their enemies radicals, but they forget these radicals are starving and lacking the medical treatment, education, and opportunities they take for granted. As Gandhi said, "An eye for an eye makes the whole world blind." The failure of Israel is the failure to peacefully meet the accusations of the original instigators—rich Arab landowners who saw the opportunity to exploit their own people to get property back to be resold again, a story that had been repeated through centuries of pogroms throughout Europe. The Israelis, had they been wise, would have recognized the disparity between the social environment they were bringing in and the existing social environment, and done everything to create positive opportunities. That means encouraging integration by treating everyone equally, winning hearts and minds. In this, they followed their European upbringing and went with a segregated community.

Allow me to digress, because I live in near proximity to several conquered civilizations, also managed in a relatively poor manner, but nothing like the Palestinians. One of these is literally a fifteen-minute walk from my home. I am referring to the American Indians. The tribes have each reacted uniquely to being conquered. The Navajos, for example, embraced the technology and are a proud people. The main difference from any rural American community and the Navajos is their race and the second culture they carry simultaneously. Some tribes traded bows, arrows, and guns for casinos, gas stations, tourism, and cigarette sales. Other tribes have faired poorly, allowing themselves to become victims, surviving on welfare, feeling sorry for themselves, helpless, and resentful toward whites. A significant difference between the Indian reservation and the Palestinians is that there is no barrier on the Indian reservation. When you pass through an Indian reservation, you often see no difference or signs of having done so; not even a street sign indicating your location. There is literally no barrier greater than the minds of the occupants, which means the opportunity for integration is there.

My point in my digression is that there are many ways to handle minorities from a government perspective, and of being a social minority. Being a minority does not mean having the lowest population per race. Being a minority means being part of a group who is not in power. Those who have and take the opportunity to embrace the new, gain immensely. Those who struggle against it or feel sorry for themselves and declare themselves as victims, are destroyed. If those in control do not provide the opportunity, they most certainly ensure their own downfall, especially if the minority is at all organized and numerous. Typically this is a result of what may be called evil, but really just boils down to selfish and hasty greed. These are shallow motives, indicating a weakness of mind, and the weak mind is prone to what appears the simplest solution: violence.

The simplest solution to grasping power appears to be through fear, which requires the perception of conflict. This Machiavellian view is self-destructive in the long run. If you want power to last, it must be gained through equal opportunity, fairness, and justice. Be cautious, as these are often professed on one hand and an illusion in the other. These also do not emerge spontaneously; they take time, effort, and faith in humanity. One cannot expect trust from another person until it is given, and anyone in a marriage will tell you, a short memory is a good thing. If somebody does something wrong, you handle the situation then and treat each new situation en nouveau, even if it is the same person. In other words, you must leave the past in the past, learn from it and move on. You cannot allow the conduct of one person to guide your views for everyone, or even that person in the future (a common source for recidivism, which is recurrent criminality). Terror works as fast as a bullet reaches its target, or a bomb levels a building. True and lasting power can take generations to build, and if it is allowed, the split second of a bullet to destroy. Do not allow a transgression to impede progress.

Conclusion

Now that we have a more clear idea of what constitutes terrorism, we can delve into the sources, reasons, and methods of international terrorism. In the next chapters we will delve into these topics. We will also examine the sources of evil, which we will see is often procedural as a part of historical patterns, and only occasionally embodied in individuals. Hopefully, by understanding the true nature of terrorism and evil, we can work together to overcome the problem of terrorism.

Taking The Red Pill

Introduction

In the blockbuster hit, "The Matrix," Neo is offered two pills. If he takes the blue pill, he forgets everything, wakes up in bed and carries on with his life as if nothing happened. If he takes the red pill, he learns the truth. There's only one catch. The only way to know the truth is to experience it, and once you have experienced it there is no turning back. Life will never be the same.

The introduction to this chapter is your opportunity to take the blue pill: simply put this book down, go back to your life, and forget the question ever came up. Once you have read this chapter there is no turning back: this chapter is the red pill, and the subsequent chapters are the reality. For me, the research to write this chapter was my red pill, my spontaneous waking in the matrix.

Like Neo, I always knew there was something I was missing. Being attentive and a trained observer, I had a good idea of reality. It was a reality I dreaded; a reality I hoped to disprove. Every time I prepare to teach political science, world geography, or recent history, I hope to find more satisfying answers. One day I was meeting with a new professor about his upcoming history class. He was still naïve, fresh from graduate school, and I was fairly new at being an academic dean. I warned him about what he would find in his preparations, and he did not believe me. Several weeks later, as his class approached the sixties, his face foreshadowed his admission: he had accidentally swallowed the red pill. He had been raped and deprived of his naivety by the evidence readily available.

Students look at the details for the sake of memorizing and passing tests. If they must speak, they either take copious notes and speak from them, or they BS and hope the teacher is either stupid or merciful. Teachers must speak extemporaneously. I liken this to being a stand-inmusician. A regular band member takes ill, so you jump in and play along with the rhythm. As a teacher, in your mind you know the story you will tell that day. When I go to my next class, I must be able to look at the syllabus and pick up my story of the day. It is no longer just a bunch of raw facts; it is a melody with a logical harmony, like a rhyming poem would be for the bards of antiquity (e.g. Sophocles). Students typically deny what does not fit into their ideal fantasy world. For that matter, even the "mature" find comfort in the blue pill, finding ways around the red pill. Ironically, they usually know much of the evidence. Now be prepared to hear what I do not want to say, but ethically must. I will start with a little quiz, provide answers and explanations, and then we will dive head first into death squads.

Terrorism Quiz

The "who" of terrorism may be treated categorically as follows: states sponsoring terrorism, terrorist organizations, and the individual terrorists. Now that we have the official definitions from the US government, let's see how much you know about state-sponsored terrorism. The American media reported each of the following acts of terrorism (and one case). See if you can identify the country (or countries) that was (were) involved or sponsored these atrocities. You will be surprised, terrified, perhaps mortified by how little you really know about terrorism. In the chapters that follow, you will observe that this list is far from complete.

1. The only nation convicted by the World Court of "unlawful use of force" aka terrorism (1986).
2. Coup d'etat in Vietnam (1963). This resulted, ultimately, in US escalation to an undeclared war that would devastate Indochina.
3. Assassinated two of its chiefs of state (1865, 1963).
4. Coup d'etat in Indonesia (1965). "Communist" supporters were rounded up and slaughtered en masse without trials. Estimates range from 500,000 to 8 million killed in these massacres. The real number is

most likely around 2 million. Most were illiterate, landless, rural farmers.

5. Mosque car-bombed in Beirut, 1985. 80 killed, 250 wounded. Almost all women and children. The actual person targeted was missed. The cleric is still alive; he never retaliated. He has higher moral standards than his attackers.

6. August 1998, bombing of al-Shifa pharmaceutical plant destroys at least half of Sudanese pharmaceuticals for both humans and animals, and all medicines for malaria, TB, and others. Only one death was initially reported (a security guard). By the next year, the death toll grew to "several tens of thousands" (Werner Daum, Harvard International Review).

7. Nicaragua violently assaulted at the cost of tens of thousands of lives to depose its chief of state (mid 1980s).

8. Cuban exiles sponsored to invade Cuba and overthrow the state (1961), and continuing to harbor, train, and give aid to further terrorist attacks against Cuba.

9. Declared "humanitarian intervention" to justify acts of aggression against other nations (two countries).

10. Use of conquest and annihilation in several states, resulting in the deaths of millions (approximately 6 million by 1987).

11. Trained and armed Afghani terrorists in the 1970s and 80s.

Quiz Answers

1. The United States, for its conduct with Nicaragua (#7), earned the prominent mark of being the only country ever convicted of international terrorism. The Security Council of the UN attempted to force compliance of all states to international law, but the US naturally vetoed the measure. The General Assembly denounced the US, opposed only by Israel and the US.

2. Henry Cabot Lodge, who lost in an election against Kennedy in the fifties, is the face behind the CIA sponsored coup d'etat in Vietnam. He is also the person who told Johnson that the real problem was in Vietnam, right after Johnson took office (Davidson, 1988, pp. 303-4). This coup d'etat occurred less than three weeks before the CIA allegedly assassinated JFK (Secret Service Agent George Hickey's kill shot was covered up and arguably accidental). Both atrocities, along with the unrelated Tonkin Gulf incidents, saved the world from greater threat of nuclear war over Europe and Cuba (JFK's focus). The entire Vietnam War, along with American terrorism around the globe, fit the "low-intensity warfare" motif of the US since the inception of the Cold War in 1945. Out of fairness to the presidents and US government, the choice was this or total global thermonuclear war. While the strategy seemed sensible during the Cold War, we are left "holding the bag" for these past crimes.

3. Abraham Lincoln and John F. Kennedy were both assassinated by US intelligence agents, though the US government would like us to think otherwise for all too obvious reasons. Our evidence for John Wilkes Booth is slim, but his affiliation with the US intelligence community is documented. When Lincoln was assassinated, the close of the Civil War was imminent. Lincoln was (and remains) the most powerful president in history because of the Civil War. There is little doubt in my mind that certain members of Congress, wanting to wrestle power back from the Executive Branch, arranged the assassination. I would not be surprised if these were the same people who began the impeachment process of Andrew Johnson, effectively defrocking the Executive Branch.

Lee Harvey Oswald supposedly resigned from the US Marines, defected to the USSR, then returned without question or delay with a Russian wife, and was involved in US-sponsored terrorism in Cuba (working with the so-called "Assets") before his involvement in the assassination of JFK. He was clearly not alone, as investigations after the Warren Commission (which itself seemed bent on proving no conspiracy to turn the heat off) show, but he was a convenient patsy. The logic of the US wanting to assassinate JFK is substantial. The intelligence community knew all too well that JFK's big interests were in Latin America (notably Cuba) and Europe. Both of these kept the US on the brink of nuclear war. The distraction of his assassination allowed American attention to be diverted to Vietnam, just as the distraction of Watergate allowed the US attention to be drawn away from Vietnam and for the Vietnamese to finally settle their own problems (namely that the Communists took power).

4. As with the coup in Vietnam, this was sponsored and organized by the CIA. President Johnson proudly announced the success of the coup to US troops in Vietnam to help boost morale. He failed to mention the mass murder of innocents of course. Indonesians today are still trying to determine the extent of the slaughter. Most victims were illiterate peasants, who were landless, making them easy targets and difficult to track.

5. The CIA executed this attack ordered by Ronald Reagan (Washington Post, 1988) against the cleric of this mosque, who was allegedly a threat to US security. It seems the President was a greater threat, as the failure to respond against the atrocity only convinced locals of American criminality, strengthening whatever opposition he had intended to quash.

6. To add further injury to the poor Sudanese, Britain refused to provide aid. The US, who launched this attack from the Indian Ocean, continues to support the embargo imposed on this nation due to a civil war that has waged since 1981, costing 1.5 million lives by 1998 (at least 2 million by now according to some estimates). The attack crippled possibility for resolution, and continues to threaten peace throughout East Africa. What do the US and Britain have against the

Sudan? Kenya borders on the Sudan, and is under the protection of Britain. Naturally, Britain wants to protect the summer vacation spot of its royals, and the US tags along for the ride. By keeping the Sudan poor and undesirable, they probably think countries like Libya will ignore the deposits of nuclear deposits they had wanted back in the eighties (before Reagan distracted them in the Gulf of Sidra, eventually bombing Tripoli). The attack on Sudan was a reaction to the attack on a US ship in a Yemenese harbor by al-Qaida. The Sudanese government had a database of al-Qaida terrorists, and two terrorists in custody that Sudan was willing to hand over to the US. The US refused, and instead chose to bomb the pharmaceuticals plant claiming affiliation with al-Qaeda. Sudan responded by releasing the terrorists. This was either an act of clear stupidity, or the US government wanted to see al-Qaeda get stronger and to undermine the Islamic government, thereby pushing the civil war on. It seems the US has adopted a posture against Islamic governments as it had with Communist governments of the 20th Century.

7. Another crime specific to Ronald Reagan, but something he inherited. The problem seems to have come to a head in 1982, when Nicaragua signed an aid pact with the USSR. Naturally the US sponsored a revolution to overthrow the government. This continued until October 1985, when the Congress stopped the financing. It resumed in 1986, only to be stopped when the Iran-Contra affair surfaced.

8. The Bay of Pigs is the best known of this atrocity, which spanned from presidents Eisenhower through Nixon. Nixon went as far as to use the same terrorists (called Assets) to attempt to assassinate Castro and Ellsberg (an American), and to handle domestic espionage, such as that against Ellsberg and the Watergate burglary. When Castro took power, the US denounced him, while the USSR offered recognition. Cuba thereby expelled US ownership of businesses in Cuba (1960), basically making the matter both financial and political. Few realize that

the reason the missile crisis occurred was because Cuba (correctly) thought the US was going to invade Cuba (the US in fact was postured to do just that, and as a consequence observed the missile movement). The missiles were intended for defensive purposes. When the USSR agreed to pull the missiles out, Soviet and Cuban troops almost came to armed conflict because the Cubans did not wish to see their defense taken away. One year later, seeing that things were not improving, American attention was diverted to Vietnam (see #3 above).

9. The US and Nazi Germany have this in common. The only instance this seems justified is in Kosovo, where a UN-led coalition was involved.

10. The US with the indigenous people of North America (millions dead), in Mexico (the US went so far as to capture Mexico City), Hawaii, and the Philippines (hundreds of thousands killed).

11. The US not only did this, but was proud of tricking the Soviet Union into invading Afghanistan (1979). As with supporting Saddam against Iran, the US turned its back on an ally when the Cold War ended. Note: both Saddam and Turkey were supported by the US with their struggles against the Kurds in the eighties. 80% of the support for Turkey's efforts of genocide came from the US. I was told once that at least the US has not turned people into soap, as Nazi Germany did. Ironically, both countries encouraged slaughter outside their borders. What happened with the bodies is another story, and frankly irrelevant. Dead bodies are dead bodies. It doesn't matter what you do with them, just that you caused them to be dead.

Death Squads

Death squads are created with the combined efforts of the CIA, AID, and Department of Defense (DOD). For a listing of US intelligence agencies, go to http://www.fas.org/irp/official.html. Training, as mentioned earlier, typically occurs at Fort Benning's School of the Americas (SOA, now WHISC or WHINSEC), but also at any other military training facility, even WestPoint. For further information on training, see the Training Terrorists chapter. This section is dedicated to death squads which have been funded, trained, and provided a variety of other supports (e.g. helicopters, databases, computer training, etc.) specifically for the purpose of terrorizing populations and suppressing opposing views to the puppet governments supported by the US (many of whom attained their power via US sponsored coups). In other words, the purpose of these groups is to retain already oppressive puppet governments. This serves a secondary function also. If the puppet government decides to go its own direction, the CIA can then easily incite a revolt, which we will discuss in later chapters.

This listing can be confusing at times, as sometimes opposing sides are simultaneously supported. Many of these groups have received training from experienced sources (e.g. Israel, South Africa, Argentina notably) at the behest of the US. The purpose of these groups is often covered by the assertion that they are combating drug trafficking, revolution (which is often justified revolution), and kidnapping. In all instances, thousands, if not tens or hundreds of thousands, or even millions have been exterminated in acts often bordering on (if not successful at) genocide (e.g. US support of Turkey and Iraq in their anti-Kurdish slaughters). As a rule, these groups do not do what they are allegedly doing, and in fact are often contributing to drug traffic, money laundering, black market organ sales, and outright blind political oppression, killing men, women, and children of all ages indiscriminately.

The largest theater of this type of US-sponsored terrorism is Latin America. Asia has also posed a major theater of operations, but not nearly as focused on, particularly regarding regime retention. El Salvador, Guatemala, and Honduras are the most documented and obvious victims. For your convenience, references are numbered and provided at the end of each section. Note: AI=Amnesty International report.

Country	Squad(s)	Notes

Angola	UNITA[1]	AI—Executed high-ranking political rivals.
Bolivia	La Mano Negra[2]	AI—3-8,000 killed from 1966 to 68. Still active in 91.
Brazil	Death Squad	Escuadron de la Muerte appeared after 1964 coup.
Cambodia	Khmer Rouge[4]	US supported 1980-date.
Chile	DINA[5]	Coup 1970-73, before, during, and after.
Colombia	Muerte A Secuestradores[6]	"Death to Kidnappers" killed 20,000 between 1986 & 94.
Cuba	BRAC[7]	"Bureau for the Repression of Communist Activities"
Dominican Republic	La Banda[8]	Began in 1965.
East Timor	Indonesian government[9]	Reports vary: 10-50% of population slaughtered.
El Salvador	Orden (later Civil Defense Corps)[10]	The main death squad, but far from alone. Others include: Ansesal, UCS, Arena, ESA, Treasury Police, National Guard, police and FAR (army) officials, MNS, Mano Blanco, UGB, to name a few.
Guatemala	National Liberation Movement (NLM)[11]	One of many to include: police, Ojo Por Ojo, Archivo, G-2, MLN, National Guard, La Mano Blanco
Haiti	Ton-Ton Macoute[12]	See also FRAPH
Honduras	Battalion 3/16[13]	Trained in Texas. Also MACHO, FUSEP, FDN, & CAL
Indonesia	Coup regime[14]	1963-1965 US trained and sponsored the coup of 65.
Israel	Duvdevan[15]	Means Cherry. US supported, they aided CIA efforts in Honduras and other Latin American countries.
Mexico	DFS[16]	Federal Security Directorate and Brigada Blanca killed hundreds if not thousands of Mexican students and activists.
Nicaragua	Contras & Sandinistas[17]	This is one of the most ironic situations. The US actually supported opposing factions simultaneously, for reasons only an insider could weasel out.

Philippines	Skull Squadrons[18]	Also the "Monkees" group, set to intimidate and murder Marcos rivals.
Puerto Rico	Police[19]	Subversive list of 150,000 "independentistas". Police death squads trained by FBI.
South Africa	Koevoet[20]	The "buffalo" battalion, responsible for assassination and sabotage of African National Congress.
Thailand	Krathin Daeng[21]	CSOC, ISOC and other agencies of the Thai government.
Uruguay	DII[22]	Department of Information and Intelligence.
Vietnam	PRU[23]	Provincial Reconnaissance Units, the Motagnards, DIOCC, and Civil Operations and Revolutionary Development Support (CORDS).

1. Washington Post, 3/14/1989, A 20.

2. Blum, W. (1986). The CIA: A Forgotten History, p.264. Washington Post, 11/25/1991, A 2.

3. Blum, (1986). pp. 194 & 240. Counterspy, 3/1973, p. 4; 5/6 1979, p. 10-11. DL, p. 238. Lernoux, P. (1982). Cry of the People, pp. 212 & 220. NACLA, 8/1974, p. 11.

4. Washington Post, 5/7/1990, A 10 editorial.

5. Atlantic, 12/1982, p. 58. Blum, (1986). pp. 194 & 240. Church Committee Report, 1976, vol. 7, p. 39. Corn, D. (1994). Blond Ghost: Ted Shackley and the CIA's Crusades, p. 251. Covert Action Information Bulletin, 8, 9, 12, 57. Counterspy, 12/1976, p. 10. Sergeyev, F.F. (1981). Chile, CIA Big Business, p. 163. Counterspy, 4/1981, p. 13. NACLA, 8/1974, p. 28. Sandford, R.R. (1975). The Murder of Allende, pp. 195-6.

6. Scott, P. & Marshall, J. (1991). Cocaine Politics, p. 261. Washington Times, 3/16/1994, p. a15. Z Magazine, 5/1994. US International Military Education and Training Program (MET) trained 6,844 Colombian soldiers between 1984 and 1992.

7. Declassified document W/1994-1995, pp. 16-17.

8. Lernoux, P. (1982). Cry of the People, p 187.

9. <u>Counterspy</u>, Spring 1980, p. 19. CIA/NSA and Australia collaborated, between 1975 and 76, in supporting Indonesian genocide. Accounts of death toll range from one in ten to half of the population exterminated.

10. Amnesty International report, "El Salvador: Death Squads-A Government Strategy" in <u>NACLA</u>. 3/1989, p. 11. Barry, T., & Preusch, D. (1986). <u>AIFLD in Central America</u>, p. 33-4. <u>Covert Action Bulletin</u>, Summer 1990, p. 51. <u>Extra</u>. Summer 1989, p. 28. House Intelligence Committee, <u>Annual Report</u>, 1/2/1985, pp. 16-19. ICC 242 referenced in Marshall, J., Scott, P.D., & Hunter J. (1987). <u>The Iran-Contra Connection</u>, p. 22. <u>LA Weekly</u>, 1/25/1990. <u>Mother Jones</u>, 1/1989, pp. 10-16. <u>New Yorker</u>, 12/6/1993, pp. 51-103. <u>Newsweek</u>, 4/5/1993. Senate Intelligence Committee Report, 10/5/1984, pp. 1-15; 7/1989, pp. 104-5. <u>Spark</u>, 4/1985, pp. 2-4. <u>The Morass</u>, p.101-2 & 133. <u>The Nation</u>, 6/5/1988; 6/7/1986, p. 793. <u>The Progressive</u>, 10/1987, pp. 15-19; 3/1986, pp. 26-30; & 5/94, pp. 20-29. UN Truth Commission cited in <u>Lies of Our Time</u>, 3/1994, pp. 6-9. <u>Washington Post</u>, 2/3/1984; 2/7/1984; 3/1984; 4/1/1984; 10/12/1984; 1/14/1985 (A20); 10/27/1989, A1, 26; & 1/4/1994 (A1, 13). <u>Washington Times</u>, 4/28/1993, A6. White, R.A. (former US Ambassador) (1984). <u>Covert Action Information Bulletin</u>, 4/1981, p. 10. <u>Z Magazine</u>, 5/1994. and at least a hundred other sources! Cost: $4-6 billion from 1980-92.

11. Barry, T. & Preusch, D. (1986). <u>AIFLD in Central America</u>, p. 21. Bass, G., & Grunow, B. (June 1993). <u>Lies of Our Time</u>, pp. 11-13. <u>CNN Headline News</u> & <u>Associated Press</u>, 3/23/1995. Cockburn, A. & Cockburn, L. (1991). <u>Dangerous Liaison</u>, p. 219. Congressman Torricelli, letter to President Clinton, 3/22/1995. Hersh, B. (1992). <u>The Old Boys</u>, p. 353. <u>Intelligence</u>, electronically published in France, 3/27/1995, p. 30. Jones, S., & Tobis, D. (eds.). (1974). <u>Guatemala</u>, pp. 202-3. Lernoux, P. (1982). <u>Cry of the People</u>, p. 186. Marshall, Scott, & Hunter (1987), pp. 133 & 193. <u>NACLA</u>, 3/1974, p. 19; 10/28/1978, p. 444; 2/1983, pp. 4 & 13; 4/17/1995; 6/5/1995, pp. 792-5. <u>New York</u>

Times, 3/23/1995; 3/24/1995, A3; 3/25/1995; 3/26/1995; 3/28/1995, A1, 6; 4/2/1995, A11. Reuters, 3/30/1995. Schlesinger, S., & Kinzer, S. (1983). Bitter Fruit 197, pp. 207-8 & 221. The Nation, 4/24/1995, pp. 547-8. The Progressive, 5/1995, pp. 8-9. Time, 4/3/1995, p. 48. US News & World Reports, 4/10/1995, p. 46. Washington Post, 1/12/1984, p. 15; 1/30/1984; 8/9/1986; 9/29/1989, A 45; 10/4/1992, A35; 3/24/1995, A1, 27; 3/25/1995, A1-3, 20; 3/30/1995, A1, 10; 4/2/1995, A29; 4/27/1995, A29. Washington Times, 5/15/1995, A13; 8/5/1992, p. A9. et al.

12. Covert Action Information Bulletin, 9/1980, p. 16; Winter 94/95, pp. 7-13. NACLA, 2/1994, p. 35. New York Times, 11/14/1993, pp. 1 & 12. The Nation, 5/3/1993, p. 580; 10/24/1994, p. 458. The Progressive, 4/1994, p. 21; 9/1994, pp. 19-26; 10/3/1994, pp. 344-48; 10/24/1994, p. 461. Washington Post, 10/9/1994, A1, 30. Washington Times, 10/7/1994, A16. Z Magazine, 6/1995, pp. 22-9.

13. Associated Press, 6/12/1995; 6/13/1995; 7/25/1995. Baltimore Sun, 6/11-18/1995; 6/15/1995. Cockburn, & Cockburn (1991), p. 225. Dillon, S. (1991). Commandos, pp. 101, 118-124. Garvin, G. (1992). Everybody Has His Own Gringo, p. 41. Intelligence Parapolitics, 9/1988, p. 8. Lies of Our Time, 3/1994, pp. 3-5. Marshall, Scott, & Hunter (1987), pp. 78-9, 132-3. Mother Jones, 4/1987, p. 48. NA, 1/23/1988, p. 85; 2/20/1988, pp. 224-5. NACLA, 2/1988, p. 15. New York Times, 5/2/1987. The Nation, 6/7/1986, p. 793. The Progressive, 8/1986, p. 25; 2/1990, p. 46. Washington Post, 1/15/1985, A12; 6/8/1988, B3; 11/28/1993, C5.

14. Blum, 1986, p. 221. Counterspy, Winter 1979, p. 27. San Francisco Examiner, 5/20/1990. The Nation, 7/9/1990, p. 43. The Progressive, 7/10/1990, p. 9. Utne Reader, 2/1991, pp. 38-9. Vatikiotis, M., & Fonte, M. (8/2/1990). Far Eastern Economic Review. Washington Post, 5/21/1990, A5; 6/13/1990, A22; 6/20/1990, A18. US supported coup to supposedly avert the "domino effect" of communism taking over

Southeast Asia. Victims were mostly landless, illiterate peasants, supposedly communist sympathizers. Estimates of death toll vary from 250,000 (based on list provided by CIA to Indonesia) to 8 million. More recent reports support the greater number.

15. Covert Action Bulletin, Summer 1988, p. 5. Intelligence Newsletter, 7/23/1992, p. 5. Israeli Foreign Affairs, 4/1989, p. 14; 2/1987; 5/1987; 2/1988; 3/1989; 4/1989, pp. 1-4; 2/20/1992, p. 3. Time, 8/31/1992, pp. 49-50. Washington Post, 8/26/1992, A14. Washington Times, 7/4/1992, A8.

16. Penthouse, 12/1989. Report on testimony of Zacaris Osorio Cruz given in Canada, regarding atrocities committed between 1977 and 1982.

17. Declassified Document, 9/1992, p. 14. The Progressive, 3/1987, p. 24. Leroux, 1982, pp 81 & 94. Terell, J., & Martz, R. (1992). Disposable Patriot, p. 149.

18. Bello, W. (1987). US Sponsored Low Intensity Conflict in the Philippines. Blaufarb, D.S. (1977). The Counterinsurgency Era, p.28. Karnow, S. (1989). In Our Image, pp. 350 & 378. The Nation, 9/19/1987, pp. 259-60. "Vigilante Terror." National Reporter, Fall 1987, pp. 24-31. Washington Post, 4/12/1984, A21.

19. NACLA, 8/1990, p. 5. Suarez, M. (1988). Puerto Rico's Death Squad Requiem on Cerro Maravilla: the Police Murders in Puerto Rico and the US Government Coverup, reviewed in The Progressive, 12/1988, pp. 40-42.

20. Briarpatch Magazine, 10/1992, pp. 55-56. Covert Action Information Bulletin, Summer 1990, pp. 63-66. Newsweek, 11/27/1989, p. 56; 9/14/1992, p. 45; 9/21/1992, p. 57. Washington Post, 6/11/1990, A18.

21. Bulletin of Concerned Asian Scholars, v9 #3, 9/1977, p. 2. Counterspy, Summer 1980, p. 14; 12/1976, p. 52. Indochina Resource Center Study, 1/1977. Syrokonski. (1983). International Terrorism and the CIA, pp. 117-8. Krathin Daeng (Red Guard) were groups of rightist students with over 100,000 members in government. Responsible for

numerous bombings, killings, shootings and harassment of labor leaders, peasant leaders, etc.

22. CID-361. Counterspy, 5/1979, p. 10. Frankovich, A. (1980). On Company Business. TV Transcript, 5/9/1980, pp. 51-53.

23. Adams, S. (1994). War of Numbers, p. 181. Blaufarb, D.S. (1977). The Counterinsurgency Era, pp. 210-11. Booth, W. "We Killed Many Vietnamese." Washington Post, 12/27/1993. Corn, D. (1994). Blond Ghost: Ted Shackley and the CIA's Crusades, p. 175. Counterspy, 4/1973, p. 22; 5/1973, p. 21. Stein, J. (1992). A Murder in Wartime, pp. 360-1. Valentine, D. (1990). The Phoenix Program, pp. 13, 126, & 259.

Argentina is noticeably missing. Covert Action Information Bulletin, Fall 1994, pp. 7-13 attributes US and CIA support to the deaths of 50,000, 30,000 disappearances, and another 400,000 Argentineans imprisoned. Apparently the 4 tons of documentation linking the US to these atrocities and atrocities in Paraguay, Uruguay, Bolivia, Brazil, and Chile were unearthed at a Paraguayan police headquarters. Amazing how thousands of deaths can be itemized in just a few lines and basically ignored by the US media. Other countries and situations are also missing, some of which will be accounted for later as we examine the history from the US position.

Conclusion

Now you have had a taste of the red pill. As we progress through the book, you will realize this was merely a snowflake on a glacier. I cannot expect you to believe, in such a short space, that the United States is such a horrible source. Frankly, I wish this list was the end of the atrocities, but it is a mere beginning. According to The Association for Responsible Dissent, an estimated 6 million people died as a result of CIA covert operations by 1987 (McCarthy, 1987). This is a mild and generous estimate that certainly does not cover all US atrocities. William Blum, a former State Department official, called this an "American Holocaust." In our next chapter we will examine how the US got involved and why.

Modis Operandi

Introduction

Modis Operandi is a criminal justice term meaning method of operation. It is literally an outline describing the way in which atrocities are committed, allowing an investigator to link crimes to each other and to the perpetrator. It is a form of fingerprint, which the perpetrator leaves behind. Here, my focus is primarily on the CIA. I will further outline why the behavior has occurred, and how that purpose has changed through the years.

Reasons

It is unfair to finger the United States as a terrorist and terrorist-sponsoring nation without an explanation as to why. There are four fundamental reasons for US-sponsored terrorism: history, politics, money, and power. I will describe each of these in detail, with the history reserved for the next two chapters. Please note: these are only reasons, and not excuses, justifications, or reasons to mitigate judgment.

Politics

How the US picks its enemies is difficult to identify. Sometimes it seems to lack reason, as with the Cold War tendency to force neutral countries to pick sides. For the most part, the United States supports any government not opposed to the US, and supportive of US economic interests within their own borders. Political ideology appears to be a secondary issue, usually ignored. The US does not seem to have any objection to dictatorships, even if those dictatorships are oppressive.

Political interests are intimately related to both money and history. From one year to the next, the US will literally switch from supporting a regime to embargo (too common to count), invasion or attack (3 successful, 4 unsuccessful), sponsoring a coup (11 successful, and a half-hearted 1995 attempt in Iraq failed), aiding or inspiring a revolution (1

29

successful, 4 unsuccessful), or assassination (3 successful, 1 unsuccessful), or otherwise forcing a regime change (6 successful). The instances listed as successful and unsuccessful are those that are known and established, and therefore, presumably, not all. The US has literally become a nation-builder, constructing governments that support US ends, and sponsoring anyone who opposes governments who are not complying with US demands (definitely directly affecting 24 countries, not counting the US).

Money

The Russian revolution ended with the formation of the Soviet Union (USSR). The "communist", or more correctly socialist, government of the USSR naturally took control of the nation's resources and focused on reconstruction. The view of the socialist is to disperse wealth evenly among the people. Naturally every country wants to monitor the amount of imports and protect its domestic industries. Unlike other economies, socialist nations have difficulty competing with foreign trade, and prefer self-sufficiency to making foreign interests wealthy at their expense. The idea of making foreigners wealthy and not dispersing that wealth among the working class is an atrocity to the socialist.

With these details in mind, it is no surprise that US relations with the Soviet Union were poor from the start. When a dictator is in power, they are only concerned about their own wealth and power. Therefore, under the Czar, Russia had been an excellent source of trade and profit for the US. Suddenly the socialist government seized all these interests, as Castro did in Cuba, immediately causing US anger. US isolationism, and the sense of security built on the idea that we are safe from military threat because of our geography, kept our military small. So small, in fact, that Holland had a larger military than the US in 1940. When the Soviets came to power, the US was in no position to do anything more than be angry.

World War II temporarily suspended US opposition to the USSR. US policy was, and basically remains: the enemy of my enemy is my friend.

The USSR and US had two enemies in common: Nazi Germany and the Empire of Japan. When the war came to a close, Patton requested to continue his assault on the Soviet troops, knowing they were our next enemy. His request was denied. US isolationism had ended, and the US was now a world power.

Immediately, US-Soviet relations turned cold, even before the surrender of Japan. Japan agreed ("acceded" as the Encarta Encyclopedia puts it, which means the same thing) to the Potsdam Conference in July, 1945 (which called for unconditional surrender). The Japanese, however, did not have the opportunity to sign surrender until September, on the USS Missouri in Tokyo Harbor. Between these two events, in August of 1945, the US government delivered a message to Moscow via Hiroshima and Nagasaki. It is no wonder that historians ignore the voices of opposition against the bombing of Hiroshima and Nagasaki, including the field commander, General McArthur, who denounced them as unnecessary. In 1946, the US Strategic Bombing Survey concurred with McArthur (Benson, 2002). Clearly Washington knew this in advance, so the only reason for it was to deliver a message. Not only were we a world power, we were the only power with the nuclear bomb. The message was simple, though implied: Don't mess with the US, or you will be next. The message was received, and the Soviets kept quiet for another four years.

In 1949, the USSR detonated the first hydrogen bomb. The Cold War was officially on. The flavor of the Cold War from that moment on was the fear of mutual destruction. Rather than face this threat, both nations turned to their allies and to third world countries to stage indirect wars. As Chomsky puts it, this was the beginning of "low-intensity warfare" (2001, p. 57), the official doctrine.

With the US as a military power, it could now stop being so isolationist, and could force itself and its monetary interests on any nation, anywhere in the world. Later, as we outline the history of regime changes, we will note that nearly all of them occurred for this reason: US financial interests.

Modis Operandi

Power

We can technically classify all Cold War-related incidents as power-related. Certainly, every incident, in one way or another, fits into power as a reason. The differences are in where the exhibition of power is directed. The majority are intended to exhibit US power and influence to other nations, and during the Cold War that meant socialist nations, particularly the USSR. Targets, during the Cold War, included supporters of opposing nations, and those who tried to stay out of the foray. Since the Cold War, it is the power to maintain US interests in foreign nations. Though the power of the US government in the eyes of the American people has also been an issue throughout this period, since the Cold War the emphasis has intensified. As we will see later, fear is power. By creating fear in the American people, the executive branch is able to gain power and hide its inadequacies.

Methods

The chain of events leading up to American-sponsored terrorist activity is fairly easy to follow. It must, however, be categorized by the type of action and the purpose of the action. The purpose of the action is always first, and since that is already covered, we need not worry about it again. The type of action is dependent on the perceived source of US grievance, and the scale of action the US feels is necessary to attain its ends. Most actions are conducted via the CIA or other US intelligence agency. US military involvement is kept to a minimum specifically to keep the atrocities undercover.

First, an enemy is identified, fitting into one or more categories to give purpose for action (history, money, politics, or power). Typically the enemy is one the people support because they intend to conduct land reform, strengthen unions, redistribute wealth, nationalize foreign-owned industry, and regulate business to protect workers, consumers and the environment. Of course these are things the US likes on paper, but only when the US profits.

Second, the opposition is identified. If the US supports the changes of the government, then the US supports the government against its opposition. As Nixon once said, the only time you like elections is when they come out in your own favor (Ellsberg, 2002, p. 108). If, on the other hand, the US does not support the changes of the government, then the US will sponsor anyone in opposition to that government, no matter where they are.

Third, support is given. The nature of this support depends largely on the resources of the party being supported. Usually it involves training and providing equipment and other resources. Seldom does it involve direct involvement by Americans. The US government does not want to be obviously involved by having Americans acting as triggermen. Like a mafia don, the US wants to keep its hands clean. The US prefers the military of foreign nations because they need the least assistance and are easily tempted by power.

Fourth, the US goes to any extreme to be sure the desired party is able to act. This means, if necessary, hiring, training, and offering any other support necessary to success.

Fifth, the victims are most commonly referred to as communists or extremists, but are really almost always peasants, liberals, moderates, labor union leaders, political opponents and advocates of free speech and democracy. Often, the destruction is widespread and distinct. The distinction is so precise, we will give it its own section in this chapter.

Sixth, the new regime takes one of two courses. They either continue to do lip service to the US, or more commonly becomes comfortable with what they have acquired and start down their own paths. When they start down their own paths, they become the new enemy, resulting in the process repeating itself. Often, the position is so powerful that the US ends up with one of two choices: ignore it or find some way to stage its end. The method for the latter includes embargo and military action, and the US would prefer to avoid the latter. Military action requires a great deal of propaganda and priming both Americans and other nations.

Seventh, when military action is required, the US begins to expose the atrocities it had supported, carefully neglecting to show itself as the source. Saddam Hussein in Iraq, the Shah of Iran, and General Noriega in Panama are prime examples. This is often called the boomerang effect.

Violence in Revolution

The CIA gives mixed messages to its trainees, in part because of the difficulty of mixing diplomacy with violence as guerrilla warfare necessitates. On one hand, they say violence should be avoided, particularly in the streets of villages. On the other hand, they realize it cannot always be avoided, so they explain how to cover up public brutality. Violence is always directed at the faction in power politically at this stage, and should be avoided among the people for the most obvious reasons: you want their support and you want recruits.

The following text illustrates the point. It is the last four paragraphs of Chapter 4: Armed Propaganda Teams (APTs) of the CIA's "Psychological Operations in Guerrilla Warfare" manual already mentioned:

As a general rule, the Armed Propaganda teams should avoid participating in combat. However, if this is not possible, they should react as a guerrilla unit with tactics of "hit and run," causing the enemy the greatest amount of casualties with aggressive assault fire, recovering enemy weapons and withdrawing rapidly.

One exception to the rule to avoid combat will be when in the town they are challenged by hostile actions, whether by an individual or whether by a number of men of an enemy team.

The hostility of one or two men can be overcome by eliminating the enemy in a rapid and effective manner. This is the most common danger.

When the enemy is equal in the number of its forces, there should be an immediate retreat, and then the enemy should be ambushed or eliminated by means of sharpshooters.

In any of the cases, the Armed Propaganda Team cadres should not turn the town into a battleground. Generally, our guerrilla will be better armed, so that they will obtain greater respect from the population if they carry out appropriate maneuvers instead of endangering their lives, or even destroying their houses in an encounter with the enemy within the town.

We should note also, in part 3, populations are instructed to reveal everything they know to the Sandinistas (of Nicaragua) about guerrilla movements. On one hand this sounds absurd. On the other, it makes the guerrillas appear legitimate in the eyes of the people. A recurring theme in the manual is transferring the perception of power from the Sandinista government to the Contra guerrillas. The following text comes directly from Chapter 3: Armed Propaganda.

3. Implicit and Explicit Terror

A guerrilla armed force always involves implicit terror because the population, without saying it aloud, feels terror that the weapons may be used against them. However, if the terror does not become explicit, positive results can be expected.

In a revolution, the individual lives under a constant threat of physical damage. If the government police cannot put an end to the guerrilla activities, the population will lose confidence in the government, which has the inherent mission of guaranteeing the safety of citizens. However, the guerrillas should be careful not to become an explicit terror, because this would result in a loss of popular support.

In the words of a leader of the Huk guerrilla movement of the Philippine Islands: "The population is always impressed by weapons, not by the terror that they cause, but rather by a sensation of strength/force. We must appear before the people, giving them the message of the struggle." This is, then, in a few words, the essence of armed propaganda.

An armed guerrilla force can occupy an entire town or small city that is neutral or relatively passive in the conflict. In order to conduct the armed propaganda in an effective manner, the following should be carried out simultaneously:

- Destroy the military or police installations and remove the survivors to a "public place."
- Cut all the outside lines of communications: cables, radio, messengers.
- Set up ambushes in order to delay the reinforcements in all the possible entry routes.
- Kidnap all officials or agents of the Sandinista government and replace them in "public Places" with military or civilian persons of trust to our movement; in addition, carry out the following:
- Establish a public tribunal that depends on the guerrillas, and cover the town or city in order to gather the population for this event.
- Shame, ridicule and humiliate the "personal symbols" of the government of repression in the presence of the people and foster popular participation through guerrillas within the multitude, shouting slogans and jeers.
- Reduce the influence of individuals in tune with the regime, pointing out their weaknesses and taking them out of the town, without damaging them publicly.
- Mix the guerrillas within the population and show very good conduct by all members of the column, practicing the following:
- Any article taken will be paid for with cash.

The hospitality offered by the people will be accepted and this opportunity will be exploited in order to carry out face-to-face persuasion about the struggle.

Courtesy visits should be made to the prominent persons and those with prestige in the place, such as doctors, priests, teachers, etc.

The guerrillas should instruct the population that with the end of the operative, and when the Sandinista repressive forces interrogate them, they may reveal EVERYTHING about the military operation carried out. For example, the type of weapons they use, ho many men arrived, from what direction they came and in what direction they left, in short, EVERYTHING.

In addition, indicate to the population that at meetings or in private discussion they can give the names of the Sandinista informants, who will be removed together with the other officials of the government of repression.

When a meeting is held, conclude it with a speech by one of the leaders of guerrilla political cadres (the most dynamic), which includes explicit references to:

The fact that the "enemies of the people" -- the officials or Sandinista agents -- must not be mistreated in spite of their criminal acts, although the guerrilla force may have suffered casualties, and that this is done due to the generosity of the Christian guerrillas.

Give a declaration of gratitude for the "hospitality" of the population, as well as let them know that the risks that they will run when the Sandinistas return are greatly appreciated.

The fact that the Sandinista regime, although it exploits the people with taxes, control of money, grains and all aspects of public life through associations, which they are forced to become part of, will not be able to resist the attacks of our guerrilla forces.

Make the promise to the people that you will return to ensure that the "leeches" of the Sandinista regime of repression will not be able to hinder our guerrillas from integrating with the population.

A statement repeated to the population to the effect that they can reveal everything about this visit of our commandos, because we are not afraid of anything or anyone, neither the Soviets nor the Cubans. Emphasize that we are Nicaraguans, that we are fighting for the freedom of Nicaragua and to establish a very Nicaraguan government.

4. Guerrilla Weapons Are The Strength of the People over an Illegal Government

The armed propaganda in populated areas does not give the impression that weapons are the power of the guerrillas over the people, but rather that the weapons are the strength of the people against a regime of repression. Whenever it is necessary to use armed force in an occupation or visit to a town or village, guerrillas should emphasize making sure that they:

- Explain to the population that in the first place this is being done to protect them, the people, and not themselves.
- Admit frankly and publicly that this is an "act of the democratic guerrilla movement," with appropriate explanations.
- That this action, although it is not desirable, is necessary because the final objective of the insurrection is a free and democratic society, where acts of force are not necessary.
- The force of weapons is a necessity caused by the oppressive system, and will cease to exist when the "forces of justice" of our movement assume control.

If, for example, it should be necessary for one of the advanced posts to have to fire on a citizen who was trying to leave the town or city in which the guerrillas are carrying out armed propaganda or political proselytism, the following is recommended:

- Explain that if that citizen had managed to escape, he would have alerted the enemy that is near the town or city, and they could carry out acts of reprisal such as rapes, pillage, destruction, captures, etc., it this way terrorizing the inhabitants of the place for having given attention and hospitalities to the guerrillas of the town.
- If a guerrilla fires at an individual, make the town see that he was an enemy of the people, and that they shot him because the guerrilla recognized as their first duty the protection of citizens.

- The command tried to detain the informant without firing because he, like all Christian guerrillas, espouses nonviolence. Firing at the Sandinista informant, although it is against his own will, was necessary to prevent the repression of the Sandinista government against innocent people.

- Make the population see that it was the repressive system of the regime that was the cause of this situation, what really killed the informer, and that the weapon fired was one recovered in combat against the Sandinista regime.

- Make the population see that if the Sandinista regime had ended the repression, the corruption backed by foreign powers, etc., the freedom commandos would not have had to brandish arms against brother Nicaraguans, which goes against our Christian sentiments. If the informant hadn't tried to escape he would be enjoying life together with the rest of the population, because not have tried to inform the enemy. This death would have been avoided if justice and freedom existed in Nicaragua, which is exactly the objective of the democratic guerrilla.

5. Selective Use of Violence for Propagandistic Effects

It is possible to neutralize carefully selected and planned targets, such as court judges, mesta judges, police and State Security officials, CDS chiefs, etc. For psychological purposes it is necessary to gather together the population affected, so that they will be present, take part in the act, and formulate accusations against the oppressor.

The target or person should be chosen on the basis of:

- The spontaneous hostility that the majority of the population feels toward the target.

- Use rejection or potential hatred by the majority of the population affected toward the target, stirring up the population and making them see all the negative and hostile actions of the individual against the people.

Modis Operandi

- If the majority of the people give their support or backing to the target or subject, do not try to change these sentiments through provocation.
- Relative difficulty of controlling the person who will replace the target.

The person who will replace the target should be chosen carefully, based on:

- Degree of violence necessary to carry out the change.
- Degree of violence acceptable to the population affected.
- Degree of predictable reprisal by the enemy on the population affected or other individuals in the area of the target.

The mission to replace the individual should be followed by:

- Extensive explanation within the population affected of the reason why it was necessary for the good of the people.
- Explain that Sandinista retaliation is unjust, indiscriminate, and above all, a justification for the execution of this mission.
- Carefully test the reaction of the people toward the mission, as well as control this reaction, making sure that the populations reaction is beneficial towards the Freedom Commandos.

The Fifth Column

In the weeks preceding the invasion of Poland, Germany sent in their so-called "Fifth Column". The CIA learned its lessons from this group's methodology of infiltration and information gathering. The following excerpt is from Chapter 4, part 5, titled: A Comprehensive Team Program - Mobile Infrastructure. Note particularly paragraphs 2, 4, and 5.

The psychological operations through the Armed Propaganda Teams include the infiltration of key guerrilla communicators (i.e., Armed Propaganda Team cadres) into the population of the country, instead of sending messages to them through outside sources, thus creating our "mobile infrastructure."

A "mobile infrastructure" is a cadre of our Armed Propaganda Team moving about, i.e., keeping in touch with six or more populations, from which his source of information will come; and at the same time it will serve so that at the appropriate time they will become integrated in the complete guerrilla movement.

In this way, an Armed Propaganda Team program in the operational area builds for our comandantes in the countryside constant source of data gathering (infrastructure) in all the area. It is also a means for developing or increasing popular support, for recruiting new members and for obtaining provisions.

In addition, an Armed Propaganda Team program allows the expansion of the guerrilla movement, since they can penetrate areas that are not under the control of the combat units. In this way, through an exact evaluation of the combat units they will be able to plan their operations more precisely, since they will have certain knowledge of the existing conditions.

The comandantes will remember that this type of operation is similar to the Fifth Column, which was used in the first part of the Second World War, and which through infiltration and subversion tactics allowed the Germans to penetrate the target countries before the invasions. They managed to enter Poland, Belgium, Holland and France in a month, and Norway in a week. The effectiveness of this tactic has been clearly demonstrated in several wars and can be used effectively by the Freedom Commandos.

The activities of the Armed Propaganda Teams run some risks, but no more than any other guerrilla activity. However, the Armed Propaganda Teams are essential for the success of the struggle.

Regime Retention

The above sections did their best to skate around the use violence. This particular manual from the CIA is intended to overthrow an existing regime, not retain an approved regime. Outright violence is a Machiavellian

Modis Operandi

solution to power, and it must be applied appropriately. It is power gained through fear. During a revolution the fear is directed toward the existing regime, with the revolutionaries acting as heroes combating that power. After the revolution, the heroes are now in power, so the people are defenseless when those heroes turn into the new tyrants. Power gained through fear comes quickly, burns hot, and then goes just as quickly. The nice thing about teaching a tyrannical regime to abuse its people is when you get tired of it you can hand the CIA's manual we have cited so frequently here to their opposition and watch the country destroy itself. Of course try to explain this to power hungry leaders and they will all think the same thing: the rule doesn't apply to me. We will, for now, reserve arguments for peaceful (without fear), lasting solutions to attaining and retaining power for our last chapter.

Since creating fear is the quickest and easiest path to power, it is exploited immediately following a successful and unjustified revolution. I qualified the statement with "unjustified" because many true revolutions did not go through this power phase. A justified revolution is arrived at by the will of the people being governed without artificial encouragement from the outside, e.g. the American War for Independence and the French revolution. The Russian Revolution remained a struggle at the onset because of competing factions (note: the American Civil War helped resolve regional issues similarly). Communist China was not formed out of revolution, but from the warring of factions, which was started by several revolutions that ultimately led to the ousting of the emperor in 1912, thirty-seven years before the communists took over.

Nixon, being the honest guy he was, once commented that an election would be nice in Vietnam only if it went the way the administration wanted it. Democracy is much like war: chaotic and unpredictable. Since the US likes to have stability in its client states, democracy becomes a paper tiger of rebel groups, which is quickly burned once they have come to power. The CIA manual encourages planting the psychological seeds of

42

democracy, but never actually talks about implementing it (available at http://barbaria.com/axisofevil/guerrilla.doc, the second is currently not available). Why? As George Orwell noted in his essays and I mentioned in the Politics chapter, democracy is a fraud to appease the masses.

Once the new power is in place it must retain its place through physical and psychological techniques the US learned from the World War II masters: Nazi Germany and Imperial Japan. These techniques have been refined, perfected, documented, and are taught at the School of the Americas (originally constructed in Panama, but since 1986 located at Fort Benning, Georgia), as evidenced by training peaks following regime changes. Critics call it the "School of Dictators" or "School of Assassins". The curriculum of this school includes: staging a coup, fixing elections, propaganda, extortion, blackmail, sexual intrigue, infiltration and disruption of opposing parties, kidnapping, interrogation, torture, intimidation, economic sabotage, and more.

Here, the fingerprint of the modis operandi is actually very easy to see, and is not hidden from the American people. In fact, it is usually the source for propaganda in advance of the seventh stage above, but is also evident while the actions are occurring, as the media loves atrocities. The most horrendous atrocities are part of psychological warfare learned at the School of the Americas, or taught by "advisors" on location. The ones I list here were learned from the Empire of Japan and Nazi Germany.

- Public or semi-public execution—when this is semi-public, the bodies are displayed in some obvious way, typically mutilated. The Japanese precedent was set in Nanking (in 1937 they killed as many as 350,000 civilians in "bayonet practice" and "decapitation contests"; Malaya, 1942, the Japanese shot 65 Australian nurses; Boas, 2002).

- Public or semi-public torture and mutilation—semi-public mutilations are combined with execution. Bodies are dismembered (hands, feet and heads are cut off), heads are put on stakes, bodies are impaled and floated down rivers (both of these best documented in Indonesia),

43

or washed up on shore purposefully so everyone can see them, particularly the media. Nanking again acts as precedent, where the Japanese raped 20-80,000 women, disemboweled or sliced off the beasts of women, and forced fathers to rape their daughters; Amboina Island, February 1942, the Japanese decapitated or bayoneted 120 Australian POWs; Philippines, December 1944, 150 American POWs doused in gasoline and burned alive; Manila, February 1945, 100,000 Philippines killed, hospital patients tied to their beds and burned, and babies mutilated and killed, their eyeballs smeared on walls like jelly (Boas, 2002).

- Mass public arrests combined with interrogation and torture—seldom do the victims survive, and when they do, and are fortunate enough to be released, they are too terrorized or brainwashed to take further action. The Nazis, starting with Krystal Nacht, best established the precedent.

- Mass disappearances and murder—People are rounded up and killed en masse, or otherwise slaughtered together (the Kurds in Turkey and Iraq for example, both of which sponsored by the US). Mass disappearances tend to become semi-public executions (Argentina, where bodies washed up on the shore without hands or heads). Again the Nazis set the precedent.

Clearly, the CIA learned a lot from the Japanese and the Nazis. In 1945, the US intelligence community began Operation PAPERCLIP. The object was to find and bring to America Nazi war criminals for their use against the USSR. Reinhard Gehlen, Hitler's master spy who had built up an intelligence network in the Soviet Union, was one of these criminals. With full US blessing, he created the "Gehlen Organization," refugee Nazi spies who reactivated their networks in Russia. These included SS intelligence officers Alfred Six and Emil Augsburg (who massacred Jews in the Holocaust), Klaus Barbie (the "Butcher of Lyon"), Otto von Bolschwing (the Holocaust mastermind who worked with Eichmann) and SS Colonel

Otto Skorzeny (a personal friend of Hitler's). The Gehlen Organization was the only source of US intelligence on the Soviets for the next ten years, most of which was fictitious. Gehlen inflated Soviet military capabilities while they were still rebuilding and recovering from the war, which inflated his importance. In 1948, Gehlen almost convinced the US to a preemptive strike, claiming war was imminent. In the 50s he produced the fictitious "missile gap" (in 1961 Ellsberg learned the truth: the US had 40 ICBMs and the Soviets had 4). Meanwhile, the Soviets successfully infiltrated his Gehlen Organization with double agents, undermining the very American security that Gehlen was supposed to protect. So much for American righteousness.

The psywar terror (or so-called "counterterror") techniques were developed by US advisors in the Philippine counterinsurgency campaign of the 1950s, and soon afterwards expanded upon in Vietnam (ref. Graham Greene's The Quiet American). The techniques were subsequently written down by Philippine psywar practitioners like Edward G. Lansdale, Charles Bohannon, and Napoleon Valeriano, and incorporated into US Army psywar training manuals. US counterinsurgency advisors were stationed in Vietnam, Colombia, El Salvador, and Guatemala by the early 1960s. The Indonesia campaign was prodigious by their standards, and basically photocopied in Argentina. Compare the following US-sponsored atrocities in Indonesia with the above list of terror tactics:

- 1961—US Ambassador Howard P. Jones' seven-point program, including "possible major psychological war campaign coordinating covert and overt resources, when proper climate can be developed."
- 1965—Indonesian Army taught psychological warfare (psywar) techniques of terror, which were then practiced in the great massacre of civilians chosen almost at random (mostly landless, illiterate peasants claimed to be communist sympathizers)
- CIA provided list of 250,000 persons opposed to the regime, who all disappeared

Modis Operandi

- Bodies dismembered, impaled with bamboo, and thrown into streams
- Heads put on pikes along the roads
- 1968, the US enlisted the assistance of Indonesian Army's psywar experts in Cambodia
- 1970, the CIA assisted Lon Nol's coup against Sihanouk in Cambodia
- 1975 (no closing date, assumed to still be happening), East Timor — Corpses displayed as part of the genocidal campaign supported and supplied by the US
- West Papua (ceded by Holland under US pressure to)—To fulfill development of one of the world's largest known deposits of copper and gold for a U.S.-dominated multinational company (now called Freeport McMoRan)

Why?

The situation of terrorism is much like the US involvement in Vietnam, which was likened to a frog in a pan. If you throw a frog in a hot pan, it will immediately jump out. If you set the frog in the pan and let it warm up slowly, the frog will not notice, and will eventually die from the heat. The frameworks of terrorism and Vietnam were in place in 1945, and had been under construction since the Treaty of Versailles (1919). Both started gradually, imperceptibly, with the US at first on the sidelines. As the US got pulled deeper into these conflicts, the situation worsened as a consequence, escalating until it could no longer be concealed from Western media. All the while, the true extent of involvement remained cloaked, and what could be seen was minimized. Both spanned multiple presidents, and both major parties. Clearly, no individual could be blamed. Vietnam spanned from FDR in 1945 to Ford in 1975, neither of who had direct involvement. Modern terrorism also begins with FDR, and given G.W. Bush's policies, will certainly carry past his administration.

The problem with FDR is more a problem of the absence of his level of leadership. Since FDR, presidents have been more controlled by the system than in control of it. The reason is simple: they have lacked the combination of vision and ability required to defy the norms they inherited and blaze their own trails toward a greater good. Though Nixon's popularity remains low, as does the assessment of his administration even by political scientists, he seems to have come the closest to achieving this balance. The problems in his case are many. He allowed himself to be drawn into the norms of secrecy with the American public. He took Ellsberg's teachings to Kissinger from the fifties (use of insanity to build power) and sixties (Vietnam) and actually applied them toward his ends, namely saving American face while getting the US out of Vietnam. He actually kept his campaign promises, it is just that his secrecy forced him to commit atrocities and to appear unethical. He broke the yoke of Vietnam, and while American attention was drawn away from Vietnam, the Vietnamese finally resolved their problems. Carter certainly entered with one vision and ended up being shaped by the hand he was dealt. Fortunately, Carter found success in his humanitarian vision after his presidency, and continues to do so today. We will discuss these matters in greater detail later.

Conclusion

Given the modis operandi, it is not difficult to browse through newspapers or books outlining recent history and see the fingerprints of US involvement. Even if the US government does not acknowledge responsibility, and the evidence is otherwise not available, it is obvious that the ultimate source is the US. It is little wonder that the US finds little love from the people of other countries, particularly those who have any clue of the US involvement in their domestic affairs. As we will see in the next chapters, many governments owe their existence to the US, and the populations of those countries and their affiliates have good reasons to hate the US.

General History

Introduction

To understand and overcome terrorism, we need to objectively understand the historical contexts in which it arose. If we follow the patterns of history, terrorism appears to be the next stage of development in warfare. At the present, terrorism appears to lie at the fringes of "civilization" in the emerging nations. As we will soon see, the central locations of terrorism have their own unique regional flavors stemming from their histories. The regions we will therefore pay attention to here include: Latin America, the Middle East, and Asia. The lack of discussion on Africa is not intended to suggest a lack of information. On the contrary, the US has pretty much left issues of Africa (south of the Moslem nations) to Europe, and really only shown significant interest in the affairs of Libya, Egypt, and the Sudan. We will begin our discussion with a little war history and an outline of the Cold War.

War History

We will see a recurring theme throughout this discussion, which are the causes of war. Many feel war is a means of solving conflict between two societies. On the contrary, war is a symptom, and the disease is simply human greed. This greed comes in a variety of forms, but will always boil down to two things: wealth and power. Draining the resources of the opponent attains wealth, whether this means war reparations, new trade agreements, exchange of property, or any number of other possibilities. In fact, making war itself is a prosperous enterprise, especially for neutral powers that provide weapons and training. Power is attained on two theaters. The powers of morale, national identity, and nationalism grow from the appearance of decisiveness (FDR), and particularly from the perception of victory. Likewise, power can be tapped by failure (look at Germany in WWI and WWII, and Japan after WWII). Power is largely a matter of how information is managed and disseminated to the population in the form of propaganda.

Warfare has changed significantly throughout the centuries. In primitive civilizations, war is a virtual ritual, used to develop male bonding, engrain cultural values, and control populations. As civilizations grew into states and then into nations, war became a sport of the nobility, who paid for their own tactical support (slaves, weapons, and other materiel). This was an age of so-called "honor". The age of honor got pushed aside by the bow and arrow, which meant hundreds of simple soldiers could be trained to kill enemies at a distance. The enemies they initially targeted were knights in heavy armor, who were unable to conclusively fight a battle of light weaponry. This is particularly significant today, because modern nations are weighed heavily by complex and burdensome technologies. Terrorists are extremely portable and virtually invisible.

The age of chivalry gradually became an age of lining up one's troops in rows and shooting from a distance. The French and Indian Wars, then the American Revolution quickly showed the value of guerillas, who would hide and shoot when it suited them rather than stand in a field like a target with a bright colored coat. The American Civil War was a virtual "total war" in which the entire population could not escape involvement. This was not a "total war" however, because targets were still military in nature. This war occurred right in the middle of the age of invention and the industrial revolution. These would not make their impact for another fifty years.

World War I (The Great War) was a war of technology. Previously, a war may see the introduction of a couple new weapons that would help turn the tide of battle. This time, each side introduced many new weapons: tanks, aircraft, poison gas, germ warfare, portable machine guns, large scale artillery, etc. The targets remained, however, military.

World War II was a war against civilians, also greatly modified by massive innovations of technology. Procedures for mass destruction, murder and mayhem abounded. In comparison, WWII was almost ten times as costly in lives as WWI. About half of the 50 million Europeans killed in the war were civilians. This was true "total war", and set the tone for every war to come thereafter: soften the support for the military by targeting specifically civilian populations. Admittedly, Germany and Japan started this earlier. Germany started in the Spanish Civil War, and Japan in East Asia. That does not mean it was right for everyone else to take it up as the doctrine for military conduct.

WWII was an awesome opportunity for FDR to make the United States a world power. Pearl Harbor brought the US out of isolation and accelerated American industry in the direction of weapons of mass destruction. Within months of Pearl Harbor, the Manhattan Project started. Clearly this was not a new idea in Washington. The political scientist portrayed in the story Fail Safe rightly attributes the bombing of Hiroshima and Nagasaki to WWIII. The reason this is true is buried in the language surrounding the incident. For example, if you look up the Potsdam Conference (July 17 to August 2, 1945) in an encyclopedia, you will see that the allies demanded unconditional surrender. The Germans had no choice. The Japanese, according to Encarta, "acceded" to the terms. This is a fancy word which a dictionary or thesaurus will quickly show means "agreed". The bombs were then dropped on August 6, just four days later, and August 9 These were more a message to the world than to the Japanese. On August 15, the Japanese government announced to its own people and the world that the war was over, they had surrendered. The treaty was signed a month later on the USS Missouri in Tokyo Harbor.

Truman became President when FDR died (April 12, 1945) just days before Berlin surrendered. Truman authorized this act of ruthless aggression. FDR clearly saw the value in scaring the war-torn world into submission at the feet of American power. He fulfilled Theodore Roosevelt's dream of US imperialism. The US then remained the unquestioned world power until 1949, when the USSR detonated their first hydrogen bomb. This led to what should be called WWIII, namely the Cold War.

The Cold War

The Cold War was a world war. Nearly every country was directly involved. Those who were not directly involved, were involved indirectly through arms sales, money laundering, or some other form of tactical support for the combatants. The common conception of World War III is that it would be a devastating nuclear war. On the contrary, the Cold War proved that a world war could be fought with the threat of potentially going "hot", namely that nuclear arms would be used between the chief combatants. Instead of direct confrontation, the two super powers (the US and USSR) and their primary allies (NATO and the Soviet Bloc) effectively redirected the conflict to third party conflicts around the world. Noam Chomsky tells us that the so-called Soviet threat was overrated and used as a means for US imperialism. Unfortunately the evidence does not refute his assertion.

Dates given to the Cold War are typically given as 1945 to 1989. In reality the Cold War lasted from the Bolshevik Revolution in 1917 until the Soviets aided the US effort in Iraq in 1990. What drove relations down was the Soviets nationalizing industrial resources and government intervention in trade. At the time, the US was distracted by World War I, during which the US military was actually rather pitiful in comparison to the latter half of the century. The US harbored strong isolationist views, so when the Great War ended, the military immediately deflated. The US government was in no condition to do anything about the animosity, so it simply sat and festered.

World War II put the Cold War on hold. At the outbreak of the war, the Nazis signed a pact with the Soviets. This pact did not make the Soviets part of the Axis, but when Germany invaded Poland in the West, the Soviet Union invade Poland in the East. Hitler got greedy and decided to push his way into the Soviet Union, which he saw as a communist state. Hitler seems to have hated Jews, gypsies, homosexuals, and communists equally. As a consequence, the Soviet Union was forced to become temporary allies of Britain, France, and of course the US.

When Patton's troops encountered the Soviets at the end of the war, he requested permission to attack. Patton knew the Soviets were the new enemy. As we already noted, the bombing of Hiroshima and Nagasaki were a message to the world of US power. The Soviet Union quietly observed this, and proceeded to do what the US and her to-be NATO allies felt was aggressive: the Soviets continued to occupy Eastern Europe rather than liberating the countries the Germans had originally captured. From the perspective of the Soviets, they wanted a buffer zone to prevent another invasion from Europe. This is understandable since France under Napoleon, and the Germans in both world wars had invaded their soil. This kept the Cold War relatively under wraps for another four years. Three events exposed the Cold War: the Soviets testing of a hydrogen bomb, the formation of NATO, and subsequently, the formation of the Soviet Bloc.

The Cold War was characteristically a protracted or limited war, based largely on fear. In support of Chomsky's thesis, we observe that Soviet "communism" was not imperialistic (likewise with other "communist nations). The Soviets actually held a defensive posture. Assuming communist doctrine is followed, communism is something that rises up from the people, and is thereby driven by the people. The implementation of communism actually sounds wonderful, so long as the rules are applied to the other guy. The Soviet system was naturally applied to the Bloc countries, with them as subject states, and therefore part of the unprivileged working class. Since the Soviets did not want another invasion, it was to their advantage to keep their buffer zone poor and undesirable to what they perceived (and perhaps rightfully so) greedy and envious Western nations. North Korea was also a subject state, treated as the spoils of war only temporarily, which will catch our attention later. Elsewhere in the world, the Soviets only gave aid upon request.

In China and Albania, the communists rose to power without Soviet aid or involvement. Neither country went out of its way to establish a meaningful relationship with the Soviets either. In fact, China armed its borders, and eventually developed short-range nuclear weapons to protect itself against the Soviets, India, and the US.

One thing most people don't realize, but should, is only the US and former European colonial powers (with the exception of Spain and Portugal) have any interest (and the capability to do something about it) in affairs outside their immediate regions. We still live in a largely regional world. So regional, that most nations are actually more concerned with their internal affairs than anything else. China is a prime example, in spite of Tibet and Kashmir. Basically, if you go around the world and look at the concerns of individual countries, nearly all are concerned with their own sovereignty and the state of their domestic economies. The only reason they turn weapons on the US and its allies is that we are interfering with these two concerns. When we examine the nature of Soviet aid throughout the Cold War, we observe that it is reactive and mindful of just these two concerns.

On the other hand, the US and her allies have consistently watched after their own interests. Most notably, the focus is US interests. So long as the US is happy, everyone is happy. Naturally this means the US is at the helm, even if this means stepping on allies. In an effort to retain a strong alliance, FDR assured France and Britain that the US would support their colonial efforts after WWII. This, of course, is a complete violation of the American perspective since the Monroe Doctrine. Truman and subsequent presidents had to grapple with the conflicting values. For example, as Japanese power evaporated in Indochina, the US transported the French to fight the Vietnamese uprising, eventually providing financing and air support until the French got tired and withdrew. On the other hand, the US

54

recognized the value of the Middle East to the American economy, and was quick to interfere with British and French attempts to attack Egypt. Not only did the US interfere, US warplanes literally faced off and forced British and French warplanes to withdraw. This was a signal to the world about who was now at the controls.

With the end of WWII, and the threat of American nuclear power, the Soviet Union reacted as could be expected: with fear. The Soviets feared invasion from the West. They also feared losing face with their own people. Their treatment of Eastern European countries was a definite atrocity, which became a key element of anti-Soviet sentiment and propaganda, but also served political interests in the USSR. We cannot forget that Stalin was an opportunist, as he showed with his non-aggression pact with Hitler, which resulted in the Soviets invading Poland from the East when Germany invaded from the West. The Berlin Crisis served its purpose as a propaganda device within the Soviet Union, but also fed into the anti-Soviet sentiment. It ended only months before the Soviets tested their first hydrogen bomb, which succeeded in warning the West of the consequences of invasion. This helped to inspire the fear of the so-called "domino effect", which we will deal with again when we discuss Asia.

Fear of nuclear war drove the nature of Cold War conflict away from the two main super powers and onto other countries of the world. While the US portrayed the Soviets as hard line imperialists, threatening to turn the world red with communism, the Soviets were in reality too soft and uninterested in imperialism. This was, in fact, the character flaw that eventually eroded the power of the Soviet government, resulting in the downfall of the USSR and the end of the Cold War. As a rule, Americans are fairly unconscious of this, simply thinking that the Soviet experiment had failed. What had failed was the Soviet ability to exploit power creation through fear. From the Cuban missile crisis, to American trips to the moon, and the constant (and accurate) perception of a reactive rather than a proactive government, the Soviet government was doomed.

General History

Chomsky and others contend that the Cold War was a front, which enabled the US to commit atrocities. Now, like Vietnam, the frog is becoming aware of the heat in the pan, because it sees the flames. The Cold War provided great camouflage, but now there is none, yet US atrocities continue.

The following chart is interesting, but does not include the World Wars, the Korean War, or the Vietnam War. Nor does it identify with Spain in the Spanish-American War (1898). It only identifies those countries known and verified to have some form of US military involvement, meaning economic weapons like embargoes and blockades are not counted (and considered by the UN and other international bodies to be among the most heinous of international crimes). It does include US occupations of former Spanish territories, Hawaii, etc. We literally watch the tide of imperial expansionism rise, fall, and after World War II shift to Cold War efforts, which only appear to be mild. This chart does not account for interventions other than military and regime-change oriented, meaning all the really bad things do not appear here. A short list of the data for this chart appears in Appendix A.

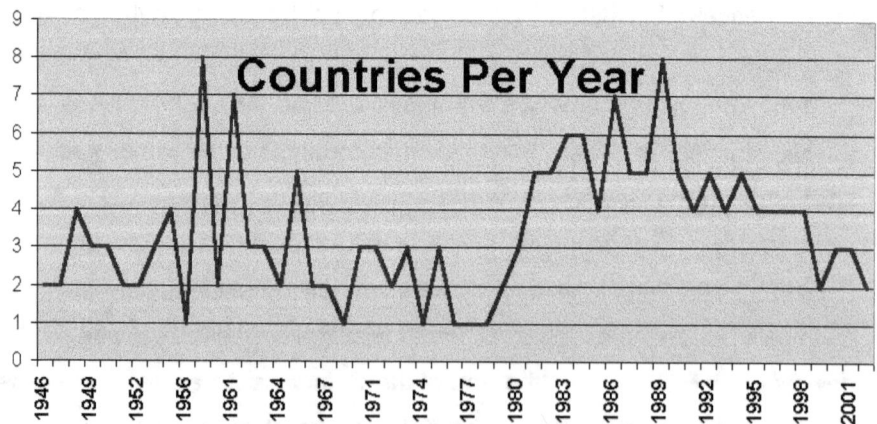

According to defense spending below, either the US has become very good at covering up the costs of its affairs, or it has found other ways to cover those costs. As US involvement in other countries increases since 1962 (ironically to include the Vietnam War), the costs have systematically plummeted. One potential reason would be nuclear proliferation. The US reached its peak in nuclear proliferation through the sixties, then needed less, and after the Cold War none. Values of 2003 and beyond are estimated per the White House under G.W. Bush. Note that the 2003 budget accounts for about $1 billion per day (3.309% of Gross Domestic Product), and does not account for the eventuality of invading Iraq. The costs of invading Iraq vary. A ground invasion and occupation for six months has been conservatively estimated to cost $100 billion if it lasts under six months (about 1% of GDP). If 100,000 troops are used to occupy, the cost is estimated at about $1 billion per week. The US only has about 293,000 deployable armed forces at any time, due to commitments literally in every corner of the globe, so it would be difficult to maintain such a show of force for any lengthy duration. Budget information is available on line at http://www.whitehouse.gov/. The information for this chart came specifically from http://www.whitehouse.gov/omb/budget/fy2004/hist.html from the hist04z2.xls file. The only other items comparable in the budget are Social Security (21.7% in 2003; which is financed separately from everything else anyway), and Health and Human Services (23.5% in 2003). Health and Human Services is interesting, considering how little we actually see of the same in the US. It would be curious to see how much of AID's funds come from there, and how much of AID's funds are used for their clandestine activities, not to claim it is entirely a front though.

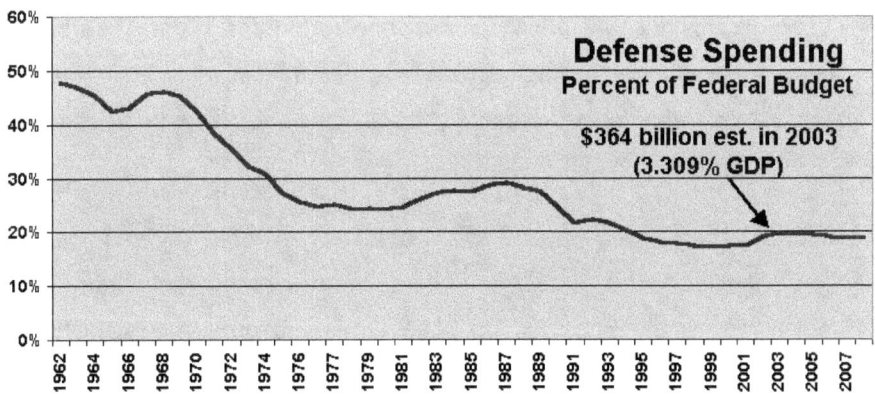

General History

The following table outlines tactics employed within ranges of years. Threat of nuclear war was one of Eisenhower's favorite things to do. JFK and Reagan both kept America (and the world) on the edge with concern that they would lead us into nuclear war, particularly JFK. The data this comes from in Appendix A does not list GW Bush's threats to use nuclear weapons as recently as 2003. Attacks here are not outright invasions, but amount to shooting down aircraft, bombings, and missile attacks. Attacks and coups were popular throughout the Cold War, and still are. We should note the nature of intervention has substantially changed also, and all forms of intervention are not accounted for, which would significantly affect the chart of involvement above.

Category	Range of Years	
Military Intervention	1890	2001
Invasion	1919	1991
Threatened Attack	1947	1958
Threatened Nuclear Attack	1950	1980
Revolt, CIA inspired	1958	1992
Regime change, forced	1965	1975
Attack	1946	2002
CIA coup	1953	2002

Asia

For simplicity, we will divide this section into four major topics: China, Japan, Korea, and Indochina. On the whole, the entire picture is based on a very long history, which we can only briefly address in this short space. We must recall that at least China and Japan justifiably claim several thousands of years history. Naturally, their views are critical to the region.

China

China claims six thousand years of history, of which at least four are easily justified. The Chinese culture is so strong, invaders found themselves rapidly sinocized (in plain terms, absorbed by the Chinese culture). Throughout its history, China has held an isolationist view. To the Chinese, outlying nations are barbaric and therefore not of interest. This is exactly the opposite of Western thought. When Westerners have thought another nation to be barbaric, they have tended to invade and sap the resources of that nation. Not so in China. So long as the barbarians mind their business, so too will the Chinese.

To give you an idea of how strong this is, we need only look back on Roman history. In the first century, China sent an embassy west to see what was going on. The embassy reached Rome. When they returned to China, they reported the barbarism they saw. China immediately severed ties with the entire west, and left them closed until Marco Polo. Even then, China remained technically closed until Portugal and Britain forced themselves on her in the nineteenth century. It is because of Chinese isolationism, and the Chinese perception of being the middle of the universe, that China was literally defenseless against Britain, when Britain decided to force opium on China in the Opium Wars. These two wars precipitated a series of revolts, destroying the power of the Emperor, starting with the Taiping and ending with the Communists. This was literally a period of various civil wars from 1848 until 1949. The Chinese attitudes, however, have not changed.

The usual response to this series of facts is the arguments on Tibet and Kashmir, not that I disagree with opposition to the occupations of these area. On the other hand, since I have expertise in Chinese history and culture, I understand their position too well. The person who poses these arguments is missing the basic demands of the culture. China is not a conquering nation, nor is it interested in subjugating peoples. It is, however, interested in retaining its sovereignty and keeping the barbarians out. To China, Tibet and Kashmir are barbaric regions bordering on an unpredictable India (with which I include Pakistan and Bangladesh). India is not India under Gandhi. Even Gandhi had difficulties keeping the very diverse population under control and peaceful. To the Chinese, the struggle of India is absurd. Had China not moved into Tibet, then India or Pakistan most certainly would have. China wants to keep as many natural barriers between her and potential barbarian invaders as possible. Tibet is nearly a perfect barrier. On one hand, I understand the Chinese, and on the other, I am sorry for the Tibetans.

We must not forget that during WWII, the US supported any power opposed to the Axis. This philosophy of "the enemy of my enemy is my friend" has repeatedly led the US to supporting combatants it probably should not have. In China, the US supported both the Kuomintang and Mao's communists, who of course were also at war with each other. This is nothing new, as can be seen looking at Yugoslavia during WWII, and more recently the Contras and Sandinistas in Latin America. The story of China shall be continued later as we discuss the Korean War, and later still as we lead up to the JFK assassination.

Japan

Japan is perhaps the most famous borrower nation in the world. It started with borrowing from China, which included the attitude toward the west. The greatest treasure the Japanese borrowed from the Chinese was Ch'an, which we know as Zen. This philosophy managed to work its way into the everyday life of every Japanese. Most importantly, it worked its way into the government, which resulted in the bokufu, or tent government, more commonly known as the Shogunates. Unlike China, Japan claims to have a single imperial lineage, which is associated with their state religion, Shinto. When Commodore Perry came in 1854 from the US to open trade with Japan, the Japanese also underwent a revolution. This was called the Meiji Restoration, the restoration of the emperor Meiji to power. The Shogunates simply lost their power, just as the Emperor of China lost his.

What is significant about the Meiji is that the Japanese found a constructive way to handle the Western intrusion. While China struggled internally, Japan sent emissaries around the world to absorb information and modernize Japan. By the end of the century, Japan was literally a power to be reckoned with, and had started expanding into Russia and Korea. By the time the US declared war on Japan, Japan had expanded to nearly unthinkable proportions. There was little in East Asia that was not under Japanese control. The Japanese had even taken the Aleutian Islands (Alaska), and were pressuring Gandhi in Eastern India. When Japan surrendered, there was a power vacuum.

Korea

Korea had the misfortune of being in the middle and at the front of the Japanese occupation in WWII. They also had the misfortune, in the end, of being in the middle of Soviet-US negotiations. They were in the middle for two obvious reasons. First, the power vacuum in the absence of Japanese occupation necessitated assistance. Second, both the US and the USSR wanted some form of retribution. Korea became the spoils of war, divided at the 38th parallel. International pressure encouraged the US and USSR to give independence back to the Koreans. Unfortunately, the liberator/occupiers brought two separate governmental ideologies and assisted, as they knew how. As a consequence, the people of Korea, while conscious of and demanding unity, faced the immediate problem of conflicting ideologies. Both North and South Korea wants a unified Korea, even today. Each wants their ideology used in the governing of a unified Korea. This became the ultimate source of conflict that precipitated in the Korean War

The Korean War was not part of the Cold War, but did eventually become an ancillary part of it. To say the Korean War was part of the Cold War would imply a confrontation between the US and USSR, and it wasn't. North Korea, while armed and trained by the USSR previously, basically acted alone when it invaded South Korea (June 25, 1950). The UN response, which was not contested by the USSR, involved 20 nations (according to Encarta: Australia, Belgium, Luxembourg, Canada, Colombia, Ethiopia, France, Great Britain, Greece, the Netherlands, New Zealand, the Philippines, South Africa, Thailand, and Turkey, with medical units from Denmark, India, and Sweden); although it is clear the US was the primary intervention force. Allied forces were immediately able to push the North Koreans back across the 38th parallel, and kept pushing north. As they drove north, China cautioned the allies not to involve Chinese territory, which basically meant staying on the Korean side of the Yalu River. As is normal under such conditions, Chinese troops were placed on the North Korean side of the Yalu to guard the border.

UN forces, which were commanded by Douglas MacArthur from occupied Japan, got greedy, pushing the North Koreans across the Yalu as ordered by Truman, and some of the forces made the serious mistake of flying sorties into China in pursuit. When UN forces reached the Yalu, they did find Chinese "volunteers" on the Korean side of the border, and confronted them. The combination made for a disaster. The Chinese responded by pouring nearly a million troops, including two armored divisions, into Korea. UN forces were crushed under what they called a human wave (1.34 million at the peak). China's objective was to keep the hostile American forces away from the Yalu River, creating a buffer zone to ensure a peaceful environment for internal reconstruction. Ideally, the PRC (People's Republic of China) wanted US forces out of Korea so North Korea could stabilize. This was not a war China wanted, as the government had only been established a year earlier on October 1, 1949. The PRC desperately wanted time to recover and reconstruct. Ultimately, even after the war was supposedly over, hostilities never ceased. As of now, 2003, the US retains a "security force" of 36-39,000 soldiers along the 38th Parallel. We civilians only think the war is over.

We should note that Truman and the American generals in the theater seriously contemplated the use of nuclear weapons. On November 30, 1950, President Truman said in a press conference: "There had always been active consideration of its [Atomic Bomb's] use...". On December 24, 1950, MacArthur submitted a list of 'retaliation targets' in China and North Korea, requiring 26 atomic bombs. Truman wanted a more peaceful solution, and because MacArthur pushed too hard, Truman fired him for insubordination. The JCS (Joint Chiefs of Staff) recommended the use of tactical nuclear weapons in 1953, which led China to begin their nuclear arms research in 1955.

At the time, no doubt fearful of US aggression, China signed a transfer agreement with the USSR to exchange technology. China terminated the agreement because of Soviet failed compliance at about the same time as the US threatened them with nuclear attack again in 1959. Chinese-Soviet relations thereafter grew increasingly cold. Then the US, under JFK in 1963, wondered why the Chinese were on the verge of detonating their first bomb. JFK, naturally wanting to retain the monopoly, threatened war if they did. China successfully exploded its first atomic bomb on October 16, 1964; launched its first nuclear missile on October 25, 1966; and detonated its first hydrogen bomb on June 14, 1967.

Indochina

In Western eyes, Indochina was nearly insignificant. For the colonial powers, and certainly for France, Indochina was strategic for trade with China. Indochina was also convenient for cheap labor and resources. These could be absorbed through a Christian aristocracy, inflicted upon a primarily Buddhist population. The power vacuum left after WWII gave the Indochinese a great opportunity to strike out for independence. The US half-heartedly supported this, and "encouraged" her ally to abandon colonialism. This encouragement included transporting and supplying French troops to Indochina, and even providing air support. At first this occurred because of FDR's agreement during WWII to help retain the alliance. Truman took this to heart, voicing anti-colonialism on one side, while running an unpopular war for the French on the other.

The US had an interest though, and it also grew a fear. During WWII, the North Vietnamese Army found support and training under Mao Tse Tung in China. At the close of the war, Ho Chi Minh immediately mobilized his people into the north and provided the resistance that would eventually drive the French out (1954). The US, supposedly driven by the red scare, did not want to see Southeast Asia fall into the hands of communism. The

US, during the Eisenhower Administration, was willing to let North Vietnam slide out of fear of another Chinese intervention. As such, South Vietnam became a puppet government guided by so-called advisors. JFK had bigger fish to fry, basically taking the opinion that national elections in Laos and Vietnam would resolve the matter without caring if those elections favored the communists. The rest of this matter, and evidence of JFK's position, we will reserve for the next chapter.

In our discussion of Indochina, we have neglected Cambodia and Laos. Later we will see references to US support of the Khmer Rouge, the premier death squad of Cambodia. The story of Laos is very different. During the "Vietnam War" this was called the "Other Theater". US airmen were decommissioned, put on the CIA payroll, and sent to fly bombing raids with retired US aircraft. That, however, is a story for someone else to tell in better detail than I can.

The Middle East

Circumstances constructed by the United States or its allies in reaction to historical events are critical to our understanding of the history of terrorism. The most prominent of these is the formation of Israel. The pressure for this peaked during and immediately after World War II. Whether the formation of Israel would have occurred or not without the events of the holocaust are not certain, as British support for Zionism seemed weak. But the holocaust seems, historically, to have created a perceived need for balance and retribution. The allies saw the atrocities of the Nazis as a reason to create this artificial country for the safety and continuation of Judaism. This is perfectly understandable, and it is easy to see how the consequences would otherwise be unforeseeable.

To understand the Middle East crisis properly, we should roll back our clocks to Moses, look at the Roman occupation, examine the Diaspora of 70 A.D. and examine the consequences on the Jewish population and the region. We should also look back to the rise of Islam, its spread, and the

64

golden age of Islam that reigned throughout the Western Dark Ages. Unfortunately we do not have the luxury of such a long-winded discussion, so we will keep this pre-history simple.

Judaism appears to be a reaction to Egyptian polytheism, which gave the Semitic peoples a simple culture and personal pride capable of simple dissemination. The Jews were foreigners in the eyes of the Egyptians, and cheap labor. As such, there was no need to make them literate, and no major attachment to them as a people. Very likely these people were at least as oppressed as any migrant group. Judaism gave them the motivation and values they needed to strike out and form their own nation, and hence the migration guided by Moses.

The Romans, centuries later, found the Middle East and Egypt relatively easy targets for their expansion. As any imperial power, they took advantage of the subject states and did their best to preserve that subjugation. In 70 A.D., in response to continual issues in Palestine, Rome decided to disperse the population (hence the name Diaspora) and force them to either leave the empire or repatriate as Romans. The Temple on the Mount was burned (a mosque is there now), and the people were forced out of Palestine. The Jews migrated as far east as China (note: the Japanese protected the Jewish settlement in Shanghai), as far west as Morocco and Spain, and north throughout Europe (particularly Eastern Europe).

European communities are known to have treated the Jews badly. Jews were not restricted from usury (lending) as the local communities were, and tended to hold education in high value. As a consequence, local populations would regularly rise up against the small settlements, in what are called pogroms, to try to create a sense of balance. The perception in these uprisings was simply that the foreigners were dominating the wealth. Ironically we will see the same idea mount after WWI. In other instances, the pogroms were driven by fear that bad crops, disease, or simply bad luck was the consequence of the Jews. Jews, by no means, are the only group to have experienced these types of hardships, but certainly carry one of the heaviest burdens of hardships throughout history, which is clearly traceable back to both Moses and the Diaspora.

Islam, upon its creation in the seventh century, appeared when Western Civilization was experiencing a power vacuum. The Roman Empire had only just disintegrated; leaving the Catholic Church behind as a shadow on the new feudal governments that would emerge. Islam was thus able to spread like wild fire throughout the Middle East, over North Africa, to Spain, and into southeastern Europe. While Islam certainly warred its way into these regions, for the most part it was a peaceful conquest. People were not forced to join Islam, they chose. Had they not chosen Islam, it would not have grown so rapidly. This ideological revolution was nothing like the Spanish Inquisition. People either chose Islam or not. Many did not, but did accept the social structures brought with it. The choice was that or civil wars and a potentially endless power struggle. Combined with the absorption of Western technologies, particularly those of Rome, Greece, and Egypt, Islam entered its golden age and everything seemed good.

Time naturally requires that power and knowledge shift. The Middle East was a pariah to the expansion and power of Catholicism. It was not that the Middle East was a real threat, but that the power of the Middle East threatened to overshadow the power of the Catholic Church. The crusades were thus inevitable for the Church to retain its stranglehold on the European population. We will see, throughout history, and in each region we examine, fundamentally the same issues, and the same two motivators for war: power and wealth. By waging a war, the ideological source gains power. The war also deprives people of resources, thereby enriching the aggressors. The problem with this model is that it inevitably collapses on itself in most tragic ways.

Let us fast-forward to World War I, the "Great War". The nations defeated in this war included the Austro-Hungarian Empire, Germany, and notably the Ottoman Empire. The Ottoman Empire spread over most of Greece, across Turkey, down through the Arab Peninsula between the Sinai Peninsula and Persia (Iran). The Treaty of Versailles (1919) was an extremely harsh end to the war, so harsh that historians all agree that it is the main source of WWII. The Treaty called for crippling war reparations, among which included the dissolution of the Ottoman Empire. France and Britain divided up the Middle East between themselves. At the San Remo Conference (24 April, 1920), France was given control of Syria and Lebanon, while Palestine, Transjordan, and Iraq were under Britain.

The British Mandate of 1922 divided Palestine from Transjordan, making Palestine a Jewish settlement area. At the time, Palestine was a virtually unpopulated wasteland. Wealthy Arabs quickly bought up property in Palestine, seeing a push for Zionism (repopulating Israel, the movement for which started in the 19th century). These wealthy Arabs then charged the Jews exorbitantly for the property. These sales were then used as political leverage to say the Jews were stealing the land from the Arabs. We should also note that the common Arab who migrated to Israel during this period was an impoverished worker following the wealth and the technology developing Palestine. Had repopulation of Israel been masterminded, like Salt Lake City, I doubt the current mess would exist. Instead, it was rebuilt bureaucratically by competing forces over decades and then forcefully thrust into existence. As a consequence, the Palestinians were neglected. Attempts for integration have been feeble at best, or overly unilateral to be effective, resulting in backlashes of terrorism whose victims have included both Palestinians and Jews.

To give you an idea of Jewish migration in the area, consider the following: 1882-1903: 25,000; 1904-14: 40,000; 1919-23: 30,000; 1924-31: 84,000; 1932-38: 215,000; 1939-47: 154,000. Jewish migration did not pose too big of a "problem" until National Socialism (the Nazis) started to encourage the Jews to leave Europe in the 1930s. The problem grew in intensity as hostility grew between laboring Arabs and the developing

67

Jewish community. Out of fear of an Axis-Arab alliance, Britain agreed to restrict Jewish migration heavily, but let Arabs move freely. This was called the White Paper (17 May, 1939). Again, we should note this is nothing new in history. In essence this is the classic struggle of the proletariat and the bourgeoisie, which has nothing to do with race or religion, but everything to do, again, with power and wealth.

As the table below illustrates, World War II led to mass illegal migration. At the end of the war, the atrocities pushed for tolerance of mass migration to Israel. The table also illustrates how the Jewish population remained a minority even after statehood. You can count on trouble in any society dominated by a religious or racial minority, no matter where they are from. We also see that Israel (roughly the size of New Jersey, which had 7.7 million people in 1990) was practically unpopulated at the end of World War I (as of 2011, Israel's population is 7.5 million).

Date	Jews	Population	% Jewish
1918	60,000	700,000	9%
1931	175,000	1,036,000	18%
1939	429,605	1,500,000	28%
1947	650,000	2,000,000	32%
1995	4,800,000	5,884,000	82%

The UN General Assembly voted to partition Palestine into Arab and Jewish states in November 1947. On the 14th of May 1948, the UN proclaimed Israel, creating the first artificial state based on a religious group. The Israeli Knesset, in July 1950) passed the "Law of Return", granting the right to Jews to migrate and settle in Israel from anywhere in the world. Migration had already exploded by this time: 1949, 239,000; 1955, 110,000; 1959, 60,000; 1965, 50,000; 1968, 40,000.

The problem, however, was not necessarily the number of people who migrated into Palestine, but the qualities they brought with them. Through the centuries, Islamic power decentralized. Their golden age decayed, and along with it many of the good core values of Islam. As education is reduced, women are the first population affected. The less educated the women, the less educated the next generation. This literally snowballs out of control, and with it individual rights. Arab migrants to Palestine were desperate, ill educated, and easily swayed by greedy members of their own society. To them, Jews were foreign devils, occupiers, colonizers, like the British and French between the wars.

Jews brought with them technology, education, and Western wealth. Of course they did not feel they were wealthy, but in comparison they were. Jews had pensions from Germany due to war reparations. Jews had support of foreign governments, particularly Britain and the US. It is little wonder this minority population appeared to horde the wealth and power, because they did. We need say no more, for people are easily envious, and will go to any extreme when they are destitute. A man with a job appears wealthy in a homeless shelter, even if he makes only minimum wage. Based on this information, we can easily see where the conflict of the Middle East comes from. This was punctuated and accentuated by the end of colonialism, the struggles of the Cold War, and the struggle for world power thereafter. Then, being thrust spontaneously on the region, naturally the neighbors were sympathetic to the Palestinians (who had migrated to Israel from their countries).

As soon as Israel was formed, its neighbors invaded it, launching a long string of senseless wars. All of this was frankly avoidable at the start without surrendering the creation of Israel. The new state was hardly in a position to deal with one tragedy when the wounds of the previous tragedy were still open. Naturally, Britain and the US had little choice but to aid them in any way they could. This was repeated several times through the nation's early years. A parent-child relationship formed, which continues to this day. Britain, like a mother, birthed this nation, and the US, like a father, has typically been the protective force. Consequently, Israel supports nearly every measure supported by the US, though the US, like any parent, is fairly inconsistent in its support of Israel (Bard, 2001).

Latin America

Unlike Asia and the Middle East, Latin America does not have a long history of issues. The issues of Latin America boil down to three things: colonialism, insurgency, and US intervention. Since the last two are related and hold special places in later chapters, that leaves little for our present discussion.

Latin America is the most terrorized region by the US in the world. Americans are nearly oblivious to the problem even though it is literally next-door. As mentioned previously, the Monroe Doctrine was basically a unilateral statement forbidding interference in the Americas by powers outside the Americas. This was clearly directed at European colonial powers. Like other colonies in the world, Latin America watched with interest the American experiment for independence. Thanks to the Monroe Doctrine and other historical events, eventually these nations gained their independence. Unfortunately, once they got their independence they had Big Brother looking over their shoulders and meddling in their affairs. Latin America is as much a buffer zone to the US, as the Bloc was to the Soviet Union. To keep these nations under control, the US sponsors anything pro-American, and pointedly destroys any opposition.

Conclusion

This chapter has basically laid out three foundations. The first foundation dealt with the nature and evolution of war, leading toward the use of terror in place of conventional warfare. Later, we will examine how and why the transition occurred. The second foundation established a basis upon which the shifting of power among first world nations drastically impacts the third world by creating power vacuums at certain times, and at others using the remaining power struggles in these nations as means toward the ends of first world nations. The third foundation is how the atmosphere of third world nations has shaped to become susceptible to terrorism and being influenced by first world countries.

Critical Mass

U.S. imperialism invaded China's territory of Taiwan and has occupied it for the past nine years. A short while ago it sent armed forces to invade and occupy Lebanon. The United States has set up hundreds in many countries all over the world. China's territory of Taiwan, Lebanon and all military bases of the United States on foreign soil are so many nooses round the neck of U.S. imperialism. The nooses have been fashioned by the Americans themselves and by nobody else, and it is they themselves who have put these nooses round their own necks, handing the ends of the ropes to the Chinese people, the peoples of Arab countries and all the peoples of the world who love peace and oppose aggression. The longer the U.S. aggressors remain in those places, the tighter the nooses round their necks will become.

Mao Tse-tung at the Supreme State Conference

(September 8, 1958)

Introduction

The atrocities here are far from complete. There are literally hundreds. The closer to the present, the more difficult it is to report on the atrocities, as the evidence becomes increasingly difficult to attain. This is evident particularly by the fact that the majority of these cases occur between 1953 and 1973. In each of these years, the US, and in particular the CIA, attempted or succeeded in overthrowing from two to six existing regimes, including its own (the instance of this is arguably justifiable, and the evidence for which is only barely becoming public).

The objective of this chapter is to illustrate why the US got involved in terrorism through understanding the processes of history. We will look at early terrorist dabbling, the lull of JFK and why, explain the why of Vietnam and the push after JFK for more indirect methods. The following graph illustrates involvement based on training. Note, <u>Time</u> linked the SOA to the death squads 4/10/1995, p. 20, and so did <u>Z Magazine</u>, 2/1994, p. 24.

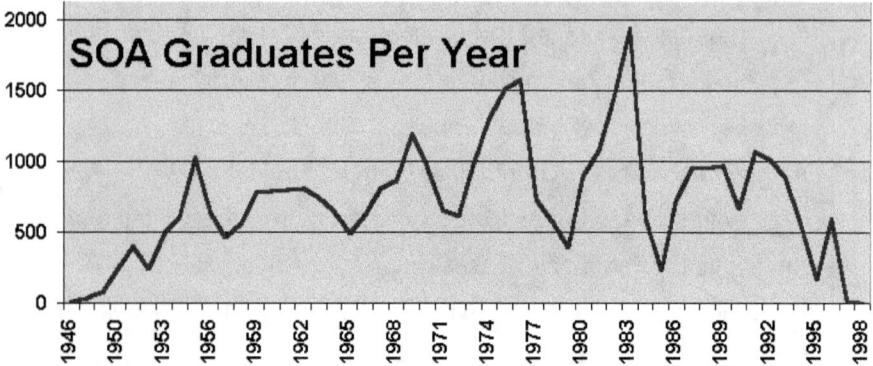

<u>Truman</u>

US involvement in international terrorism was relatively insignificant before JFK. The School of the Americas (SOA, now WHISC) got its start on Truman's watch. Truman seemed to have a relatively hands-off approach toward his policies with "lesser" nations. By this I mean he did not seem to be so interested in kicking off another violent conflict, at least not until Korea. The following table outlines the two known instances of interference in other countries. Given the proximity in time to WWII, his initial reaction was probably fairly well justified. These basically amount to regime retention and learning.

1947	**Greece** — President Truman requested military aid to Greece to support right-wing forces fighting communist rebels. For the rest of the Cold War, Washington and the CIA would back notorious Greek leaders with deplorable human rights records. See also the coup of 1967. **Operation MK-ULTRA** — Inspired by North Korea's brainwashing program, the CIA began experiments on mind control. The most notorious part of this project involved giving LSD and other drugs to American subjects without their knowledge or against their will, causing several to commit suicide. Funded in part by the

	Rockefeller and Ford foundations, research included propaganda, brainwashing, public relations, advertising, hypnosis, and other forms of suggestion.
1948	**Italy** — The CIA corrupted democratic elections in Italy, where Italian communists threatened to win the elections. The CIA bought votes, broadcasted propaganda, threatened and beat up opposition leaders, infiltrated and disrupted their organizations. The communists were defeated.

We should note other events that were critical during his administration. For example, the surrender of Nazi Germany, the Potsdam and Yalta Conferences, Japanese surrender, the bombing of Hiroshima and Nagasaki, the formation of the UN, the Nuremberg Trials, the return of France to Indochina (with Truman's support, even literally paying them to keep the war going), the Berlin Crisis and Airlift, NATO, the rise of the Iron Curtain, Communist China (PRC), the formation of Israel, the first invasion of Israel by the Arab League, the H-bomb tested in the USSR, the Occupation of Japan, the Korean War, threatening China with a nuclear attack... On the home front, the civil rights movement started to raise its head and roar, and Truman actually paid attention. Other events at home included unprecedented prosperity, dismantling of the OSS (1945) and creation of the CIA (National Security Act, 1947), the Office of Policy Coordination created in 1948 (a covert wing of the CIA responsible for "propaganda, economic warfare, preventive direct action, including sabotage, anti-sabotage, demolition and evacuation procedures; subversion against hostile states, including assistance to underground resistance groups, and support of indigenous anti-communist elements in threatened countries of the free world."), Operation Mockingbird (CIA recruited at least 400 journalists and 25 news agencies, including ABC, NBC, CBS, *Time, Newsweek,* Associated Press, United Press International, Reuters, Hearst Newspapers, Scripps-Howard, and Copley News Service), unprecedented generosity to war-torn Europe, the Red

Critical Mass

Scare and McCarthy...This was quite a busy time. Compared to FDR's administration, this one seemed even more trying. This list alone shows how, during Truman's administration, entangling alliances formed, and the stage was set for conflict throughout the rest of the century and into the next.

The only thing that is missing from the list is what happened when the US first came into Germany. US troops rounded up German scientists and spies (see Modis Operandi chapter). The US wanted the scientists for many reasons. Germany had labored to develop many new technologies including: genetics, jet propulsion, ballistic missiles and other rocket technology, nuclear energy and weapons, chemical and biological weapons, not to mention the progress they made in anatomy at the expense of European Jews, gypsies, homosexuals, and communists. The Soviets did the same thing.

The affect of rounding up the spies was quite profound. Of course the spies were wanted war criminals, who had to justify their existence just to be saved from trial and summary execution at Nuremberg. Unfortunately, they were the only source of intelligence the US had on the USSR until the early sixties. The consequence was a steady stream of lies about Soviet capabilities, which persisted through Eisenhower's administration. This stream of lies resulted in what came to be known as the "missile gap". Daniel Ellsberg was, at the time, working on nuclear strategy for the Rand Corporation on contract for the Pentagon. When the truth was finally unveiled during JFK's term, it was a shock: the USSR did not have hundreds of missiles, they had four ICBMs (inter-continental ballistic missiles)! Meanwhile, the US had forty and had backordered 1,600 more to compensate. Considering JFK's stance, which we will soon develop, there was no way that backorder would be canceled on his watch.

Eisenhower

One of the ironies of Truman is the "Truman Doctrine." Basically the position of this statement was that the US would extend the Monroe Doctrine to include any country in the world, particularly if that country was combating potential communist take over. Where Truman only seemed to apply this in Korea, with catastrophic results, Eisenhower aimed for less risky frontiers. In the following table, bolded dates are used to indicate successful violent regime changes that clearly occurred because of Eisenhower. Dates that are not bolded were failures. There is only one instance in our list that was "peaceful" (in other words they did what we told them to do), which was Ecuador in 1961. We should note that events between 1961 and the end of 1963 actually occurred while JFK was in office. It appears the actions of the CIA commenced into JFK's administration until he put a stop to them and redirected their attention elsewhere. The only reason this seems true is the obvious two-year hiatus.

1953	Iran–A CIA-sponsored coup overthrew the democratically elected Mohammed Mossadegh, after he threatened to nationalize British oil. The CIA replaced him with a dictator, the Shah of Iran, whose secret police, SAVAK, are compared to the Gestapo. US-Iranian relations plummeted when the Shaw was ousted by the Ayatollah Ruhollah Khomeini in 1979 while the Shah was in the US for medical treatment.
1954	**Guatemala** —A CIA-sponsored coup overthrew the democratically elected Jacob Arbenz. Arbenz threatened to nationalize the Rockefeller-owned United Fruit Company, in which CIA Director Allen Dulles owned stock. Arbenz was replaced with a series of right-wing dictators whose bloodthirsty policies killed over 100,000 Guatemalans in the next 40 years.

1954 to 1958	**North Vietnam** — CIA officer Edward Lansdale spent four years trying to overthrow the communist government of North Vietnam. The CIA also attempted to legitimize a tyrannical puppet regime in South Vietnam, headed by Ngo Dinh Diem. These efforts failed to win the hearts and minds of the South Vietnamese because the Diem government, besides being Catholic, was opposed to true democracy, land reform and poverty reduction measures. The CIA's continuing failures resulted in escalating American intervention, culminating in the Vietnam War. See also Greene's The Quiet American.
1956	**Hungary** — Radio Free Europe incited Hungarians to revolt by broadcasting Khruschev's Secret Speech, in which he denounced Stalin. It also hinted that the US would aid the Hungarians in their fight. This aid never came, dooming the revolt, which resulted in a major Soviet invasion. The conflict killed 7,000 Soviets and 30,000 Hungarians.
1957 to 1973	**Laos** — "The Other Theater" was so top secret, US correspondence was not allowed to reference it by any other name, and air force pilots were reclassified as civilians who flew in antiquated equipment. The CIA waged this secret war, with up to 50% casualty rates among pilots, 400 Americans died in combat, and another 400 MIA, against the Geneva accords of 1962. They sought to overthrow the democratically elected Pathet Lao, a leftist group with enough popular support to be a member of any coalition government. In the late 50s, the CIA even created an "Armee Clandestine" of Asian mercenaries to attack the Pathet Lao. After suffering numerous defeats, the US started bombing, dropping more bombs on Laos than all the US bombs dropped in World War II. A quarter of all Laotians eventually became refugees, many living in caves.

1959	**Haiti** — The US military helped "Papa Doc" Duvalier become dictator of Haiti. He created his own private police force, the "Tonton Macoutes," who terrorize the population with machetes. They killed over 100,000 during the Duvalier family reign, and the US did not protest.
1961	**Dominican Republic** — The CIA assassinated Rafael Trujillo, a murderous dictator supported since 1930 by Washington. Trujillo's crime: his business interests grew so large (about 60 percent of the economy) that they began competing with American business interests.
	Congo (Zaire) — The CIA assassinated the democratically elected Patrice Lumumba. Public support for Lumumba's politics ran so high the CIA could not clearly put his opponents in power any other way. Four years of political turmoil followed.
	Forced Regime Change—**Ecuador** — The CIA-backed military forced the democratically elected President Jose Velasco to resign. Vice President Carlos Arosemana replaced him, with a new VP of the CIA's choice.
1961	**The Bay of Pigs** —Planned in 1959 by Eisenhower in response to Castro nationalizing sugar plantations. The CIA sent 1,500 Cuban exiles (called Assets) to invade Cuba. "Operation Mongoose" failed, due to poor planning, security, and no air support. This was the CIA's first public setback, causing President Kennedy to fire CIA Director Allen Dulles. The Assets would continue to be used through the Nixon administration for a variety of dirty tasks (terrorist attacks from Southern states, notably Florida, on Cuba, in which Lee Harvey Oswald participated; attempted assassinations of Castro and Ellsberg; the break-ins at Ellsberg's psychiatrist's office and Watergate), and probably beyond.

Critical Mass

A few incidents occurred on Eisenhower's shift that deserve attention. For example: the end of open hostilities in the Korean War, threats of nuclear attack on China (1953 and 1959), the Warsaw Pact (1955), the beginning of Chinese research in nuclear weapons (1955), the U-2 incident (1959), Che' Guevara's death, and Castro's takeover in Cuba. Comparatively speaking, Eisenhower experienced a relatively mild presidency. On the other hand, American fears continued to escalate due to the Cold War, and the Civil Rights Movement began to build momentum with Rosa Parks and Brown versus the Board of Education.

JFK

JFK was driven by a sense of ethical and moral duty not typical in history. It began with his father's public exhortation of isolationism in Europe. FDR fired him and effectively ended his political career. His narcissism knew no bounds, so he passed his ambition to the willing Joe Kennedy. When Joe was killed, JFK was the inheritor of that ambition. Not only was it an imposed ambition, his father made it clear that he was sub-adequate—a last resort. His father effectively bought his campaigns and did underhanded deals to win at any cost. JFK was not pleased but was obedient until one of these dealings with a mob boss threatened his presidency. He was ethical in many regards, especially with fulfilling his duties of office. Feeling inadequate and not wanting to be there, he had no personal ambitions, so he dedicated himself to making the world a better place—namely eliminating organized crime, the civil rights movement, and avoiding war.

JFK did not just avoid war, he waged peace. He did such an effective job of waging peace, that even this author believed for a long time that he was a very dangerous president bent on the destruction of the USSR and China. This perception is quite understandable even for a historian because the era was filled with such animus that every politician is assumed to be a cold warrior. He wasn't typical politician though, especially since he had narrowly survived his ship being sunk by the Japanese. Such an incident has a profound effect on a person—death and destruction are no longer just abstract ideas. The typical peace-loving president uses the Just War Theory (last resort, minimal force, etc.) as a guideline. Politicians habitually over-intellectualize and aim for moderate language. When it comes to matters of war and peace things are very simple. Ask any lieutenant in the field, any police officer intercepting an armed felon, etc. JFK understood the need for decisive words and action as tools of deterrence.

Negotiation is done by communicating with words which is not possible when everyone is dodging bombs and deafened by cannon fire. War is not a matter of negotiation among civilized peoples, it is a struggle between barbaric civilizations. Unfortunately that is the only language less developed civilizations know, the way tyrants hold onto power, the people take that power back, and empires oppress weak nations. With all the capabilities today, there is no excuse for nations to maintain large standing armies when an international force with real authority could keep relative peace—as was the purpose of the League of Nations and now the ineffectual UN. Nations too have egos to prevent this surrender of power and to put them where they don't belong—and JFK certainly understood this. He was clearly for non-interference, but realistic without the extreme isolationism of his father. He was too deep for LBJ, the DOD, etc. to really understand him then, and difficult even today. What follows below contradicts everything just stated because it follows the more conventional interpretation of him and the Vietnam War.

JFK was a big game hunter. He capitalized on American fear and focused on Cuba, Eastern Europe, and China. This heightened focus is the most likely source of his assassination. While the US did involve itself in lesser matters around the world in 1961, these seem to come to an abrupt halt before 1962. Through 1961, American focus was redirected to the Soviet and Chinese "threats". Part of JFK's plan was to reach the moon by the end of the decade (which was accomplished). The significance of this is immeasurable. Not only did this improve American morale, it would ultimately provide further damage to Soviet decay. From the military development perspective, the mission in space was critical to perfecting global tactical weapons.

The Bay of Pigs turned into a massive fiasco. First, the US trained and planned the mission using Cuban "Assets", who were exiles opposed to Castro. They were promised air and tactical support. In the end, they were abandoned, probably because JFK really wasn't that interested in Cuba in the first place. The fiasco, of course, looked really bad. Then the Berlin Wall went up, and JFK had to save face somehow. Therefore, in 1962 he tried to compensate by staging a US invasion of Cuba. US forces amassed around the Caribbean in preparation and started flying spy planes over Cuba. Observing the American threat, Castro turned to the Soviet Union. The Soviets responded by sending short-range nuclear missiles in hope this would dissuade US aggression. A US spy plane observed the missiles, which resulted in the thirteen-day Cuban Missile Crisis. This standoff put the whole world on the edge. If JFK's objective was to at the least damage one big game animal, he succeeded. Khrushchev's authority was significantly undermined by this particular event, even though Khrushchev gained disarmament of Turkey in exchange.

1963 was clearly a fated year. With the missile crisis barely over, relations with China continued to slide. Chinese research in nuclear weapons was moving in leaps and bounds, and it was obvious. It had to be extremely obvious to the intelligence community that China was on the verge of testing a nuclear bomb and not far from ICBM and hydrogen bomb capabilities. I find no specific details about why the threat occurred, but given this, it is the most likely reason JFK threatened China with nuclear war not long before his assassination.

On November 2, 1963 (less than three weeks before JFK's assassination), Henry Cabot Lodge aided a military coup that overthrew the Diem government (pronounced Zee-ehm). Reasons for this are not very clear, but it did pave the way for outright American involvement in South Vietnam. At the time, the US, North Vietnam, and its own Buddhist community pressured South Vietnam. The Buddhists were protesting, and monks were burning themselves alive in protest of not being able to openly practice Buddhism. Destroying the Diem government effectively drove the South into chaos, as any power vacuum will. The Buddhists, thinking the communists under Ho and Giap were their friends, became highly militant. These were the VC (Viet Cong), formed in 1959; the common person-turned guerilla in South Vietnam. The Vietminh (aka NVA) did their best to avoid direct conflict. The idea was simple: let them kill each other, then come in and declare a victory. It took until 1975, but the strategy ultimately worked.

Clearly, JFK's saber rattling over China's nuclear program, the Cuban Missile Crisis (precipitated by a planned full-scale US invasion of Cuba), and the solidifying of the Iron Curtain in Europe, most certainly scared those who were "in the know." It is thus little surprise that he needed to be eliminated and American attention needed the diversion of the much safer matter of Indochina, which brings us to our next topic. Judging by JFK's position on Laos and Vietnam (basically letting them go) and his behavior with China, the Soviets and Cuba, he was a "big game hunter" and therefore a threat to national security. No member of the intelligence or military community wanted a war with China. Everyone feared the "human wave". For evidence, merely look at Johnson's conduct in Vietnam.

Hoping to raise American aggression to invade Cuba, JFK's top brass came up with Operation Northwoods. The plan was to stage terrorist activities on Americans, including hijackings, bombings, plane crashes, and, of course, dead Americans. He rejected the plan. What is significant about this, is that the DOD would have the nerve to expose something like this to the President. It is easy to believe that former presidents may have been clueless about the actual nature of the outcomes when they gave orders. If the DOD felt they could discuss such matters directly, then clearly JFK knew of other such activities and had not rejected them. His reasoning was logical also. Compare the two notions: the US causes a hundred thousand foreigners to die versus the US causing five Americans to die. Which do you think will be on the cover of every newspaper faster? The latter of course. The former might result in a truth commission and a belated apology, but the latter will result in months of scandal unraveling. JFK was wise to reject the plan, but it most likely did not help his already damaged image in the eyes of the DOD and the intelligence community, who would see this as a way to accelerate their objectives.

The Assassination

Let us quickly eliminate the term conspiracy from our vocabularies. The reason is simple: conspiracy tends to be associated with personal gain. The assassination of JFK does not appear to be for personal gain, but rather to prevent a hot WWIII that loomed during his presidency. Frankly, it worked. Some, particularly those who lived through it, will argue that Lady Bird may have caused this to happen because she was so power hungry. I seriously have my reservations and suspect George Hickey's accidental shooting was the actual cause of death. From what I see of the US-Vietnam atrocity and the JFK assassination, these saved many more millions of lives than it affected. That, of course, does not justify the sufferings of the South Vietnamese.

We note a number of incidents leading to JFK's death that make it stand out: Oswald defected to the Soviet Union, the Berlin Wall (1961), Bay of Pigs (1961), Oswald was readmitted without question and with a Soviet wife, US preparation to invade Cuba leading to the Cuban Missile Crisis (1962), Oswald's involvement with CIA sponsored Assets in Texas (aka US trained Cuban terrorists), Chinese nuclear arms development and JFK's threat (1963), JFK's general focus on Eastern Europe and Cuba, and the Diem coup staged by Lodge. We note a number of other incidents immediately following his death: the immediate silencing of Oswald, China's atomic test, the solidifying of the Iron Curtain in Europe, and the immediate diversion of American attention to Indochina.

The assassination has raised eyebrows for four decades. Several commissions have been assigned to investigate, and none have come close to answering the critical questions. There were clearly at least two gunmen, most likely three. Oswald appears to be a convenient patsy, who was shot by Jack Ruby, a mobster from Las Vegas, before he could say anything. Jack Ruby died of cancer in prison, saying he would take the story with him to the grave. He did just that. Of course this and Oswald's obvious involvement with the CIA has fueled conspiracy theories galore. If we put it that way, then we must also chalk this little discussion up as a "conspiracy theory" in spite of my recommendation to avoid the word conspiracy. This "conspiracy" prevented war with both China and the Soviet Union, which would have clearly had devastating affects on the entire planet. Given the facts, what do you think you would have done in the position of US military leaders and the intelligence community?

Johnson

There is speculation that Lady Byrd or Johnson himself may have had a hand in the assassination of JFK. While they may have had great expectations, I seriously doubt the allegation. First, had Johnson staged this, he would have been more assertive. On the contrary, his behavior was that of a frightened man, as we shall soon see. My personal suspicion is that he, at some time, got an idea about why JFK was assassinated, and watched out that the next funeral wasn't his. After rediscovering JFK (top of JFK section) we can re-examine LBJ and see the two as partners. Like Andrew Johnson after Lincoln, LBJ attempted to continue the policies of his predecessor. LBJ's failure was in waging peace—but that is no easy feat to accomplish. His failure and the manipulations of Henry Cabot Lodge et al are the real cause of US extended involvement in Vietnam, fitting the perceptions outlined here as a prevention of global thermonuclear war and/or another war with China.

Two days after JFK was assassinated, Lodge, who staged the coup, visited the now President Johnson. "If Vietnam is to be saved, you, Mr. President, are going to have to do it," he said. Johnson replied, "I am not going to lose Vietnam. I am not going to be the president who saw Southeast Asia go the way China went." This comes from Phillip B. Davidson, a devout soldier and member of the US MACV supervising the war. If that isn't a wake-up call, I don't know what is. Also, in case you didn't know, Lodge is infamous around the world. To-date, he cannot leave the US without first verifying that wherever he goes won't extradite him to somewhere else where he will be tried for war crimes. His name is a rash across Latin America also.

Johnson lacked the support to do much with Vietnam for over nine months. He was also concerned with the upcoming election. Wisely, he redirected attention to the economy with his Fair Deal program, and the media had its hands full with the Civil Rights Movement. Meanwhile, the North Vietnamese were struggling to convince the US to abandon their mission in Vietnam. One could also argue that they wanted the US in to help erode the abilities of South Vietnam and the Viet Cong, but this appears unlikely. The first Tonkin Gulf Incident, in early August 1964, was not enough to motivate Congress to act. A few days later another incident occurred. This was the day Ellsberg began working directly for the Pentagon. He was assigned the task of filtering all information on Vietnam. He had no sooner started his shift when the messages started to pour in. Apparently several American ships found themselves in a storm in the Tonkin Gulf at night. Radar anomalies led them to believe they were being fired on from several directions. Without verifying the information, the fleet started shooting back. Frankly, I would love to have seen this from a distance, because there were no other ships around. Anyway, the messages kept pouring in for hours. Finally somebody got a bright idea:

there were no explosions, no casualties. They stopped firing and sent a message back reporting they weren't sure they had ever been attacked. It didn't matter. Johnson used this as an excuse.

Within hours, US bombers were over North Vietnam retaliating for something that literally never happened (which was verified repeatedly later). The next day, Johnson managed to get Congress to pass the Tonkin Gulf Resolution. In Johnson's words, he described it as being like "grandma's blanket, it covers everything." Basically the resolution gave him free reign to war in Vietnam without formally declaring a war. Meanwhile, he was campaigning for office claiming he would not increase US involvement in Vietnam. At the same time he was ordering troop deployments.

With few exceptions, Johnson's war in Vietnam was contained within South Vietnam. The reason was simple. He was terrified that China would intervene if they invaded North Vietnam, or even extended the war. Johnson, as a consequence, appeared weak to military leaders, whose concern was not so high, at least not in Vietnam. Johnson had mass media and the Civil Rights Movement working against him too, even though he was supportive of the movement. The movement made the whole government look bad, and justifiably, they were right. Uncertain how to handle the media on Vietnam, Johnson basically neglected it. Basically, the entire situation backfired on him at home. The perception of the population was that he had pushed the US into Vietnam without public approval, and that his efforts in Vietnam were indecisive. At the risk of being a Johnson apologist, he was actually over-decisive. Instead of giving control to the military to fight their own war, he literally called every shot. His failure to adequately use the media, and his fear of Chinese intervention combined to make him appear inadequate. As Davidson says, we won the battles but lost the war. In some respects, I beg to differ with Davidson. If you consider the objectives of the Vietnam War, the US technically won. So what were those objectives?

Critical Mass

Kennedy wanted Vietnam to hold public elections and decide its own fate, just as Laos had (Bobby Kennedy verified this just before his assassination). If our hypothesis about JFK's assassination is correct, then those behind his assassination wanted US attention diverted. This objective was achieved. Second, Johnson wanted to contain communism, so the North would not overrun the South. This was also accomplished during his term. When we get to Nixon, the objectives changed again, but that's a whole new story.

Since Johnson was avoiding big game hunting (which killed JFK), he focused on all the little game. All of a sudden, US training of terrorists, sponsorship of death squads, regime changes and coups skyrocketed. The following table outlines US international atrocities (regime changing, retention, etc).

1964	**Brazil** —A CIA-sponsored coup overthrew the democratically elected government of Joao Goulart. The junta that replaced it, over the next two decades became one of the most bloodthirsty in history. General Castelo Branco created Latin America's first death squads (CIA trained), or bands of secret police who hunted down "communists" for torture, interrogation and murder. Often these "communists" were no more than his political opponents.
1965	**Indonesia** —A CIA-sponsored coup overthrew the democratically elected Sukarno. The CIA had tried to eliminate Sukarno since 1957, using everything from attempted assassination to sexual intrigue, for nothing more than his declaring neutrality in the Cold War. His successor, General Suharto, massacred between 500,000 and 8 million civilians accused of being "communist", though they were illiterate, landless peasants. The CIA supplied the names of countless suspects (approx. 250,000). The number killed remains uncertain. **Congo (Zaire)** —A CIA-sponsored coup installed Mobutu Sese Seko as dictator. The hated and repressive Mobutu exploited his

	desperately poor country for billions. **Greece** — With the CIA's backing, the king removed George Papandreous, a prime minister who failed to vigorously support US interests in Greece. **Dominican Republic** — A popular rebellion broke out, promising to reinstall Juan Bosch as the country's elected leader. The revolution was crushed when US Marines landed to "uphold" the military regime by force. The CIA directed everything behind the scenes.
1967	**Greece** —A CIA-sponsored coup overthrew the government two days before the elections. The favorite to win was George Papandreous, the liberal candidate (see 1965). During the next six years, the "reign of the colonels"— backed by the CIA—ushered in the widespread use of torture and murder against political opponents. When a Greek ambassador objected to President Johnson about US plans for Cypress, Johnson told him: "Fuck your parliament and your constitution." **Operation PHEONIX** —The CIA helped South Vietnamese agents identify and then murder alleged Viet Cong leaders operating in South Vietnamese villages. According to a 1971 congressional report, this operation killed about 20,000 "Viet Cong."
1968	**Bolivia** —A CIA-organized military operation captured legendary guerilla Che Guevara. The CIA wanted to keep him alive for interrogation, but the Bolivian government executed him to prevent worldwide calls for clemency.

Other events during the Johnson administration include the Ramparts Affair (1966) and Operation CHAOS (1968, as part of the Vietnam War). *Ramparts* began a series of unprecedented anti-CIA articles on CIA payoffs at universities (e.g. University of Michigan and MIT) to train South Vietnamese, and revealed that the National Students' Association was a CIA front, recruiting students through blackmail and bribery, including draft deferments. Operation CHAOS, though started in 1959 under Eisenhower, was boosted by LBJ. CHAOS was a CIA operation to spy on Americans (7,000 individuals and 1,000 organizations) searching for Russian instigators using student radicals.

Nixon

Frankly, before I started investigating the history of Nixon and the Vietnam War, I thought Nixon was a liar and a jerk. After my research, my opinions have completely reversed and I am inclined to see him as an unsung hero of humanity. You're about to see why.

Nixon actually kept his campaign promise to get the US out of Vietnam. He had a humongous obstacle though. He had to make a good show and be able to declare a victory to the world, and preserve American honor in Asia. In these objectives, he succeeded. At the risk of sounding like a Nixon sympathizer, his strategy was ingenious and most likely masterminded by him and Henry Kissinger alone. Unfortunately, documentation of this masterpiece is missing, and for good reasons. On the other hand, Daniel Ellsberg was such a good record keeper, that he actually has the full explanation but may not realize it, so allow me to explain.

In the late 1950s, Ellsberg gave some lectures on WWII, particularly the use of insanity as a political device in international affairs. Kissinger attended these lectures. Years later, Kissinger told Ellsberg that everything he (Kissinger) knew about Vietnam, he had learned from Ellsberg. Again, years later, as Nixon's right-hand man, Kissinger made a similar comment, only he said everything he knew about publicity and international politics he learned from Ellsberg. Ellsberg, in his book <u>Secrets</u> (2002), observes this, then goes on to observe Nixon's putting on a show of insanity (the pink golf cart episode). He fails, however to make the next connections, though he also documents them.

When Nixon took office, he immediately did several things. First, he set up a system for propaganda. He knew the media had devoured Johnson. For a full discussion of this system, see my book At War With the White House. Nixon was a diplomat, and used this skill wisely, combining what he knew of the orient (which was a lot) with the teachings of Ellsberg. The media was immediately under control. Nixon then turned the war over to the Pentagon. Unlike Johnson, who called all the shots, Nixon let the Pentagon do their jobs.

The military immediately steps up the war. More troops are deployed, the theater is expanded to include Cambodia, Laos, and North Vietnam. Nixon's professed strategy was "hit hard and pull out fast." Boy did he hit hard (and in 74, pulled out fast). As the war is getting stepped up, Nixon immediately goes on a tour of China and Moscow. Somehow I cannot find any information about what was specifically said at these meetings, but that is not surprising. Even though I cannot find it, I can put myself in his shoes. Nixon is simply telling them what he plans to do and asks them to simply step back and let him do it. To the American population, Nixon appears to be a liar. He wasn't, just as he said. In fact, he had a tendency to be painfully honest (e.g. "Your vote doesn't count."). Having reviewed many tapes of him, and knowing the history well enough to put myself in his place, I see absolutely no evidence that he lied about anything...literally. He is remarkably believable and has, within reason, a trusting character.

Following this course of events, the war wages on under virtual wraps. Nixon begins to distract America with other matters. Where Johnson allowed everything else to dominate him, Nixon grabbed the bull by the horns. He implemented the welfare system, food stamps, and declared a war on drugs, which our table below shows that he did just that. From his perspective, and American popular opinion's perspective, Nixon did many great things. Unfortunately he delegated the tasks in the table below to

Critical Mass

what computer geeks call hackers, because they are ruthless about how they achieve their objectives.

1969	**Uruguay** —CIA-sponsored Dan Mitrione convinced right-wing forces to use torture as a routine, widespread practice. "The precise pain, in the precise place, in the precise amount, for the desired effect," was his motto. His death squads would rival the Nazis, leading revolutionaries to kidnap and murder him a year later.
1970	**Cambodia** — In 1962, Congress ineffectively cut off CIA funds for its secret war in Cambodia. In 1970, the CIA overthrew the highly popular Prince Sahounek, who wanted to keep Cambodia out of the Vietnam War. He was replaced by Lon Nol, who immediately threw Cambodian troops into battle. This unpopular move strengthened once minor opposition parties like the Khmer Rouge, who would later be supported by the CIA when they achieved power in 1975 and massacred millions of their own people.
1971	**Bolivia** —A CIA-sponsored coup overthrew the leftist President Juan Torres, after half a decade of CIA-inspired political turmoil. In the next two years, dictator Hugo Banzer had over 2,000 political opponents arrested without trial, then tortured and executed.
1973	**Chile** —The CIA assassinated Salvador Allende, Latin America's first democratically elected socialist leader. The problems began when Allende nationalized American-owned firms in Chile. ITT offered the CIA $1 million for a coup (reportedly refused, for obvious reasons). The CIA replaced Allende with General Augusto Pinochet, who tortured and murdered thousands of his own countrymen in a crackdown on labor leaders and the political left.

Nixon managed his routine of insanity in politics so well, he got himself re-elected. His second election was a victory in his objective with Vietnam. Here is the logical reason why. The Vietnamese, watching the ruthlessness of the Nixon administration, no-doubt hoped another weakling like Johnson

90

would get elected. When that failed to happen, they could only see four more years of massacres. Up to this point, their willingness to negotiate was negligible. All of a sudden there is an agreement between the NVA and the US. The NVA and US will exchange POWs every fifteen days for a period of sixty days. During this period, the US is to completely withdraw from Vietnam, and in exchange the NVA promises to stay out of the South. Also, in the middle of this sixty day period, Watergate bubbles up to the surface (like this type of stuff is new in history). Nixon announces that he knew nothing about Watergate, and most likely he that was true at the time it happened. It was mighty convenient though. A few months after the withdrawal, he resigns from office on threat of impeachment. Ford becomes President and immediately pardons Nixon. Awful suspicious, but then it only gets better. US attention is immediately drawn from Vietnam. The next year nobody paid attention when North Vietnam overran South Vietnam. By 1977, the Buddhist monks were burning themselves in protest of Communist oppression (communism is treated as a religion, and we all know how religions can grow jealous of each other).

Post-Nixon

As usual, after a high-profile president, low profile presidents come in. Ford, like LBJ, focused mostly on saving his own head. Carter was a lot more gutsy, but seemed uncertain what to do with the tide when he was given the controls. While atrocities dropped during the Carter administration, he never did get a complete handle on the situation. He became most effective as an ex-president, and continues waging his peaceful campaign today.

This particular period could be called the "Death of Heroes" period. This death begins with Nixon and Watergate, culminating when Ford pardoned Nixon for all crimes known and not known. Immediately everything related to the Federal government came under scrutiny. Calls were made to reinvestigate everything, including the assassination of JFK.

Critical Mass

Ford and Carter had a tightrope to walk with absolutely no sympathy from the population. The population wanted nothing to do on the foreign front, but both presidents had to deal with the mess of the past two decades.

In 1974, Pulitzer Prize-winning journalist Seymour Hersh published a story about Operation CHAOS, the domestic surveillance and infiltration of anti-war and civil rights groups in the US. The story sparks national outrage. In the same year, Congress held hearings on the illegal domestic spying efforts of James Jesus Angleton, the CIA's chief of counterintelligence. His efforts included mail-opening campaigns and secret surveillance of war protesters. The hearings result in his dismissal from the CIA. Meanwhile, the House of Representatives cleared the CIA of any complicity in Watergate. To grapple control of the President, Congress passed the Hughes-Ryan Act, requiring the president to report non-intelligence operations of the CIA to the relevant congressional committees in a timely fashion.

1975 saw a wave of attacks and scrutiny against the CIA. Victor Marchetti and John Marks published "The CIA and the Cult of Intelligence", a whistle-blowing history of CIA crimes and abuses. Marchetti spent 14 years in the CIA, eventually becoming an executive assistant to the Deputy Director of Intelligence. Marks spent five years as an intelligence official in the State Department. Philip Agee, who worked in covert operations in Latin America during the 60s, published "Inside the Company" detailing CIA crimes in which he took part a diary of his life inside the. These books sparked public outrage leading to the "Church Committee" investigation. The investigations led to a number of reforms intended to increase the CIA's accountability to Congress, including the creation of a standing Senate committee on intelligence. However, the reforms proved ineffective, as with the Iran/Contra scandal, showing the CIA can easily control, deal with or sidestep Congress. This was not helped when President Ford created the "Rockefeller Commission" to whitewash CIA history and propose toothless reforms. The commission's namesake, Vice President

Nelson Rockefeller, was himself a major CIA figure. Five of the commission's eight members were also members of the Council on Foreign Relations, a CIA-dominated organization.

Meanwhile, the CIA kept busy proselytizing American capitalism at the expense of local populations, as the following table illustrates.

1975	**Australia** —The CIA helped topple the democratically elected, left-leaning government of democratically elected Prime Minister Edward Whitlam. They gave an ultimatum to John Kerr, the Governor-General (appointed by the Queen of Britain). Kerr, a longtime CIA collaborator, exercised his constitutional right to dissolve the Whitlam government, never before exercised. **Angola** —Henry Kissinger launched a CIA-backed war in Angola. Contrary to Kissinger's assertions, Angola was a country of little strategic importance and not seriously threatened by communism. The CIA backed the brutal leader of UNITAS, Jonas Savimbi. This polarized Angolan politics and drove his opponents into the arms of Cuba and the Soviet Union for survival. Congress cut off funds in 1976, but the CIA was able to run the war off the books until 1984, when funding was legalized again. This entirely pointless war killed over 300,000 Angolans.
1976-1983	**Argentina** —August, 2002: 4,677 declassified documents show Washington (notably, Kissinger) closely collaborated and offered support to a military dictatorship responsible for the deaths of at least 30,000 Argentines, most of them workers and students, called a "war on terrorism".
1978	**Latin America** —"Operation Condor," organized collaboration between the secret police of Argentina, Brazil, Chile, Uruguay, Paraguay and Bolivia to capture and execute political opponents across national borders. Each of these regimes had overthrown constitutionally elected governments with the active collaboration of the CIA and US State Department. Opponents were kidnapped

	and "disappeared" in combined transnational operations, which included the use of death squads to assassinate opponents anywhere in the world. Kissinger is wanted by courts in Argentina, Chile, Spain, France and several other countries to answer for his role in plotting military coups that toppled Latin American governments and for other atrocities. He cannot travel abroad without first receiving guarantees that he will not be extradited.
1979	**El Salvador** — An idealistic group of young military officers, repulsed by the massacre of the poor, overthrew the right-wing government. However, the US compelled the inexperienced officers to include many of the old guard in key positions in their new government. Soon, things were back to "normal" — with the military government repressing and killing poor civilian protesters. Many of the young military and civilian reformers resigned in disgust. **Grenada** — Coup headed by Maurice Bishop overthrows first prime minister, Eric M. Gairy. **Nicaragua** — Anastasios Samoza II, with his murderous and hated personal army called the National Guard, the CIA-backed dictator, fell. The Marxist Sandinistas took over, and they are initially popular because of their commitment to land and anti-poverty reform. He lived in exile in Miami, Florida, then in Paraguay where he was assassinated in 1980. The Guard became the Contras, who fought a CIA-backed guerilla war against the Sandinista government in the 1980s. **Afghanistan** —The CIA immediately began supplying state-of-the-art weaponry to any faction willing to fight the occupying Soviets, including fanatical Muslim extremists like Bin Laden, and Sheik Abdel Rahman. Such indiscriminate arming assured civil war when the Soviets withdrew.
1980	**Iraq** — With US encouragement, Hussein invaded Iran in 1980.

During this costly eight-year war, the CIA built up Hussein's forces with sophisticated arms, intelligence, training and financial backing. This cemented Hussein's power at home, allowing him to crush the many internal rebellions that erupted from time to time, sometimes with poison gas. It also gave him all the military might he needed to conduct further adventurism — in Kuwait, for example.

El Salvador —Oscar Romero, Archbishop of San Salvador, begged Carter, "Christian to Christian," to stop aiding the military government slaughtering his people. Carter refused, and shortly thereafter Roberto D'Aubuisson had Romero shot through the heart while giving Mass. The country dissolved into civil war, with the peasants in the hills fighting against the CIA and DOD supported government. CIA-trained death squads roamed the countryside, committing atrocities like El Mozote (1982, see http://www.soaw.org/new/article.php?id=43 for 767 of the roughly 1000 victims). By 1992, some 63,000 Salvadorans were killed.

At the end of this period, while on a trip to the US for medical attention, the Shah of Iran was ousted and replaced by the Ayatola. This was embarrassing because the CIA had put the Shah in power in the 50s. His regime was a long time CIA puppet, which gave rise to Moslem fundamentalists who were furious at the CIA's backing of SAVAK, the Shah's bloodthirsty secret police. In revenge, the Moslems took 52 Americans hostage in the US embassy in Tehran. This episode did not end until Carter was on his way out of office.

Reagan-Bush

Reagan is hailed as the "great communicator." He was good at getting the public to pay attention to what he wanted, and retained good publicity in spite of many very damning issues. One of these was his economic policy affectionately called Reaganomics, often called the "trickle down theory." This policy looked good on paper to the rich, which of course made Reagan look good to the wealthy and powerful. The lower and middle class saw this as a way to make the rich richer.

After examining the economic methods of the rich, my conclusion is that Reaganomics was nearly the equivalent of doing nothing while looking like he was doing something. Looking like you are doing something is important, even if that something is inherently or perceptually bad. The reason trickle down adds up to nothing is simple. The rich invest their money before taxes, thereby protecting their wealth from taxes. The lesser classes, on the other hand, spend on products that are actually liabilities, like homes with 30-year mortgages, cars that depreciate, etc. As a consequence, the lesser classes are taxed more because of their behavior. Due to the nature of economics for the rich, there is no way to adequately tax them under the Robin Hood scheme of taking from the rich and giving to the poor. If you want the rich to give to the poor, create investment opportunities for them. If you want to rescue the poor from the "rat race" of their lives, teach them financial literacy, as Kiyasaki recommends in Rich Dad Poor Dad.

With American attention diverted to the economy, Reagan then brought out his "Star Wars" program. The idea of this was to devise a defense system in outer space to defend against incoming Soviet ICBMs. American attention was then drawn away from the economy and onto the threat of the Soviets. He was then able to redirect attention again. This time the target was smaller countries supposedly under Soviet protection. As with the Nazi and Fascist propaganda in the Spanish Civil War, the Soviets were implicated for something they had little to no involvement in until they were called upon for assistance because the victim had nowhere left to turn. Reagan and Bush could then move forward as Cold War warriors and retain great public opinion ratings. That is, until the fall of the Soviet system in 1989.

In 1986, Southern Air Transport was exposed as a CIA front, because Nicaragua shot down a C-123 transport carrying supplies to the Contras. Eugene Hasenfus, the lone survivor, turned out to be a CIA employee, as were the two dead pilots. This exposed the Iran/Contra scandal of Reagan also. Congress held hearings, and several key figures (like Oliver North) lied under oath to protect the intelligence community. CIA Director William Casey died of brain cancer before Congress could question him. Reagan managed to escape relatively unscathed by this scandal, as did Bush.

1981	**Iran/Contra Begins** — The CIA began selling arms to Iran and using the profits to arm the Contras fighting the Sandinista government in Nicaragua. Reagan vowed the Sandinistas would be "pressured" until "they say uncle.'"
	Nicaraguan Contras — "Support" was given to the anti-Sandinista contra guerillas. CIA provided them with the <u>Psychological Operations in Guerrilla Warfare</u> and <u>Freedom Fighter's Manual</u>. The <u>Freedom Fighter's Manual</u> includes instruction on economic sabotage, propaganda, extortion, bribery, blackmail, interrogation, torture, murder and political assassination. Support included arming fighters in Honduras and aiding them in their incursions into Nicaragua, eventually led to the US earning the prestigious title of being the only nation ever convicted of International Terrorism by the World Court (1986). In spite of this, Congress pulling the funding (Boland Amendments, 1984), being denounced by the General Assembly of the UN (voted against by the US and Israel, and in one instance also by El Salvador), and apart from the veto override the US exercised, also being denounced by the UN Security Council, the US continued its support covertly at the cost of tens of thousands of lives. UN-backed investigators found that US counterinsurgency forces killed 90 percent of an estimated 200,000 civil war victims.
1983	**Grenada**—A boomerang coup and Bishop's murder were followed

	by an invasion by US troops and a contingent from the Organization of East Caribbean States on October 25. **Honduras** — The CIA supplied military officers with the *Human Resource Exploitation Training Manual,* teaching them how to torture people. Honduras' notorious "Battalion 316" used these techniques, with the CIA's full knowledge, on thousands of leftist dissidents.
1985	**Beirut** —The CIA coordinated the car-bombing of a mosque, timed to detonate when the service ended to maximize casualties. 80 died, 250 were wounded, most were women and children. The Moslem cleric who was targeted was missed. The Washington Post finally reported the real source of this catastrophe in 1988.
1986	**Haiti** —The popular revolt in Haiti made "Baby Doc" Duvalier "President for Life". The U.S., not liking instability in a puppet country, flew the despotic Duvalier to the South of France for a comfortable retirement. The CIA then rigged the upcoming elections in favor of another right-wing military strongman. Violence kept the country in political turmoil for another four years. The CIA tried to strengthen the military by creating the National Intelligence Service (SIN), which suppressed popular revolt through torture and assassination.
1989	**Panama** —The US invaded Panama to overthrow a dictator of its own making, General Manuel Noriega. Noriega had been on the CIA's payroll since 1966, and had been transporting drugs with the CIA's knowledge since 1972. By the late 80s, Noriega's growing independence and intransigence angered Washington.
1990	**Haiti** —A CIA-sponsored coup overthrew Jean-Bertrand Aristide. Aristide, a leftist priest, had competed against 10 comparatively wealthy candidates, captured 68 percent of the vote, and held office for only eight months. The subsequent military dictators brutalized the country, as thousands of Haitian refugees escaped

	the turmoil in barely seaworthy boats. As popular opinion called for Aristide's return, the CIA began a disinformation campaign painting the courageous priest as mentally unstable.
1991	**Iraq—The Gulf War**—The US liberates Kuwait from Iraq. Iraq's dictator, Saddam Hussein, was another creature of the CIA and DOD, empowered by the coup of 1968 (likely CIA sponsored).

With the fall of the Soviets, Bush needed new targets to build his popularity on. Panama offered a solution in the drug war. Haiti was an embarrassment he dared not publicize. Then Hussein had bad timing. Had Hussein invaded Kuwait before 1989, he would have been supported. Now, with the Soviets out of the picture, Bush needed somebody to pick on. Hussein was instantly convenient and timely. We should not pretend that Hussein is anything of a nice guy. History, however, shows that Hussein's timing was simply bad and created an opportunity for a president who was rapidly failing on the home front to try and salvage support for the election of 1992. It was not enough, because Clinton won handily.

Clinton

Earlier we discussed the ever-changing face of warfare. Clinton began to seriously exploit economic warfare. Now that the Cold War was over, it became increasingly difficult to directly assault other nations. The rise of the Internet in the early 1990s opened the doors to world communication. All of a sudden, the CIA could not keep up with all the leaks. Like Tom Thumb, the CIA had worked diligently to cover its problems. Unfortunately for them, there were too many holes to logistically cover. On the flip side, there were immediately so many leaks (e.g. the manuals in 1996) that the CIA could count on only one defense: too much information. Now, if you want information on the military or the CIA, everything you want is readily available. Much of it is even put on line by the DOD and CIA. If you wander around looking at the military training and procedures manuals, you quickly find yourself buried in codes and doublespeak. There is literally too much information even for a committee to wade through. They have literally discovered a way to have secrets by having none.

1993	**Haiti** — The chaos in Haiti grew so bad that President Clinton had to remove the Haitian military dictator, Raoul Cedras, on threat of US invasion. The US occupiers did not arrest Haiti's military leaders for crimes against humanity, but instead ensured their safety and rich retirements. Aristide was returned to power only after being forced to accept an agenda favorable to Haiti's ruling class.
1995	**Iraq**—The US encouraged Iraqi military commanders to stage a coup, promising support. Five hours before the planned attack, the US informed the commanders that there would be no support, behaving much as they had at the Bay of Pigs. Iraqi officials became aware and arrested thousands. We should note that US and British bombings of Iraq did not stop after the Gulf War, but have persisted even to the present (2003). The cost of life in Iraq is in the millions. At least a million infants alone have lost their lives due to the embargo and lack of resources, such as lack of drinking water kept in place by US and UK attacks.
1998	**Somalia** —In August, the US bombed the al-Shifa pharmaceutical plant, destroying at least half of Sudanese pharmaceuticals for both humans and animals, and all medicines for malaria, TB, and others. Only one death was initially reported. By 1999 the death toll grew to "several tens of thousands" (Werner Daum, Harvard International Review).

Clinton's biggest crime was frankly not giving the media enough dirty laundry to make money. As a consequence, the Monica Lewinsky ordeal and the Whitewater Scandal punctuated his terms. He significantly reduced military spending, and reversed the economy working toward a balanced budget. He was absolved of any involvement in Whitewater. As far as Lewinski, if you are to crucify him for that, you better do the same with most former presidents, many, like FDR, highly respected. Frankly these scandals are an atrocity of the US media. This is not to say Clinton was an angel. As we get closer to the present, it is increasingly harder to find information because what the US doesn't want you to know, they aren't telling. It is obvious, however, that Clinton maintained many of the threads left by his predecessors, particularly in the Middle East and Latin America.

GW Bush

Since this is current history, I will only say this: DON'T BELIEVE WHAT I SAY, FIND OUT FOR YOURSELF. This is the same message I give to political science and history classes. I do not expect my audience to believe me. I want them to discover the information for themselves and see the reputability of the sources for themselves. You cannot believe everything you read. This was a key message of Orwell. You certainly cannot believe all the sources out there. However, when the sources become overwhelming, names, dates, and reputable sources are provided, you can follow-up and see the real facts. They are not pretty. Once you have discovered for yourself, then I will pass on the recommendation given by Thoreau in his Civil Disobedience: Cast your whole vote.

Before 9/11, GW Bush was being railroaded out the door of Washington. His approval ratings were clearly in the toilet, and everything he tried was immediately wrong. 9/11 became an opportunity for him (and Juliani) to get approval ratings. In spite of reinstating Reaganomics (discussed above), his approval ratings are still impressive. Americans are all too willing to buy into whatever propaganda shows their elected officials are good. At present, there is plenty of media damnation of the administration and all its policies, which dare not show on prime time or on the front page of newspapers because Americans don't want to hear it. This, in fact, is a critical problem in American society. For detailed timelines of the 9/11 incident, see http://www.viewzone.com/911.html and http://vander.hashish.com/articles/ 911/timeline.html. These and other timelines and articles can be found on a search of Google (CIA invest 9/11), which turns up over five thousand documents.

Let us examine circumstances around 9/11. Why would Bin Laden want to attack the US? Two major reasons: first to get the US to invade Afghanistan and thereby save the country from its enormous poverty level (since the US pulled support when the Soviets left). Use the attack to inspire Moslems around the world to rally against their governments for supporting the US, and thereby undermine the already decaying governments of the Middle East (which Bin Laden wants overthrown anyway). The Attack accomplished both of these objectives.

The details provided by the timelines, and the fact that Bin Laden has not been captured, are additional indicators that the US had interests in the 9/11 attacks. Why would the US allow 9/11 to occur? The answers are simple: money and power. I need not go into the details of insider information, CIA investments, etc. showing profit margins resulting from the 9/11 attacks. There is plenty of information on the Internet already. All you have to do is look. Bush had the opportunity to get a UN investigation, which was refused, and UN assistance, also refused, which further imply that there is cover up going on. Instead, Bush decided to go with our junior partner, Britain, virtually alone. The world community tolerated this, but the world community was not thrilled. This set the stage and precedent for Bush's next target: Iraq.

In the months leading up to the attack, Bush was working heavily to improve his oil investments and prepare for war. The week before the attack, on September 4, 2001, I was lecturing a class on the Vietnam War. We started to talk about current events and I pointed out the US was readying for a major war. Needless to say, the attacks only confirmed my point. The information was public knowledge, available through numerous media sources. The day of the attack, my mother called and said, "This is the big one you predicted." Students made the same assertions. My answer shook them: "Not this one, not yet. We still have another two years." It doesn't take rocket science to follow the patterns. Bush needed a war, and he wanted one with Iraq even before he took office. Afghanistan wasn't Iraq, but it did offer public approval ratings and international support. It also offers an oil pipeline opportunity Cheney will profit from. Bush is willing to make any sacrifice for his power and wealth, even sacrificing relations with US allies like Germany and France, but that is another story. America has pretty well bought into his propaganda and little war, so only history will be able to answer all the allegations thrown at him now. Very likely, short of impeachment, we may not know for at least one generation, which is the norm.

Before the dust has settled over Afghanistan (in fact fighting continues but is not publicized), Bush turned his attention again on Iraq. While the world community agrees that Hussein is a problem, they seriously question the motives. Iraq is virtually crushed by US and UK bombardment, embargo, and no-fly zones already. One sure sign that something is wrong is that the US has resorted to trying to pay off neighbors (e.g. Turkey) to stage the invasion. Bush has also gone so far as to damn anyone opposed to his objectives, including the long-standing allies of France and Germany. Germany specifically refers to itself as a friend who is disagreeing. One economist claims the US will be a third world country if it doesn't invade Iraq. More likely, an invasion of Iraq could result in the US destroying relations with its own allies, and consequently becoming a third world nation. American arrogance neglects the fact that it is by far not the only super power, and not alone in having economic weight to throw around.

2001	**Eritrea—** US-sponsored coup thwarted.
2002	**Afghanistan**—US supported forces (Northern Alliance) in the slaughter of 3,000 alleged Taliban; followed later by invasion claiming pursuit of Bin Laden (who hid in Pakistan), and occupation without end with few possible reasons: an unlikely oil pipeline, support of opium production and the defense industry. **Venezuela—** US-sponsored coup thwarted by the civilians of

	Venezuela. Venezuela is the number one supplier of oil to the US. The result of this US plot: gas prices have skyrocketed.
2003	**Iraq**—Invasion over alleged Weapons of Mass Destruction (given by US and used to fight Iran in 1980s) and non-existent al-Qaeda affiliation. Really a massive scandal to privatize infrastructure and resources, block oil, and promote US defense industry.

Post-Script and Obama

Evidence suggests complicity of the Bush administration in the terrorist attacks of 9/11, that the attacks were known of and allowed to happen. Bush overtly wanted war with Iraq even during his candidacy. The reasons were economic, and the policies continued into Obama's administration. The real reason for the war in Iraq was destabilizing oil competition; a theme carried through in Libya and indirectly in Syria. The war in Afghanistan appears to have two purposes: an oil pipeline and restoring opium production. This is a system of economics by catastrophe (see Naomi Klein's Shock Doctrine) with the added benefits of imposing police-state tactics, promoting the defense industry, privatizing public services, imposing austerity by cutting other public services, while retaining domestic solidarity. This is basically a wish fulfillment of oligarchs going far beyond anything envisioned by the Reagan administration.

Obama appeared to have good intentions coming into office. Inexperience, naivety, and not having the courage of conviction led to him adopting the policies and many of the personnel of Bush. Where he did try to make a difference, he compromised his ideas into worthlessness and failed to lead by setting new goals. He basically became a puppet of the right. His naivety continues to show in his foreign policies that crush economies, destroy national identities, and create anti-American identities that inspire foreign "terrorist" organizations. Beware though that terrorist is now the term used to describe only foreigners who stand up against imperialism and has nothing to do with actual violent behaviors. You do not win hearts and minds with bombs or police state tactics, you win enemies willing to take up arms against you. Your enemies are not defined by the color of their skin, national origin, or religion. Real terrorists come from every social group, and are at least as numerous and dangerous in the United States as anywhere else. You don't fight terrorism and win. You win over terrorism by opting out of the game of winning at all costs.

Real terrorism is the resistance to imperialism by those who cannot meet imperial aggression in open conflict. Foreign terrorists would not exist if the United States did not act as such an aggressor, and honestly cannot typically reach our shores. The real threat is a domestic policy that enables predatory foreign policy. Domestic policy is so oppressive that the real threat is right-wing domestic terrorists. People do not resort to radical affiliations without cause. Desperation, an environment of blatant lies, inequality, injustice, and hopelessness are certain causes. It is literally only a matter of time before the empire collapses from within. If the world were wise, it would embargo the United States, seizing and nationalizing assets of oligarchs, the World Bank, and International Monetary Fund responsible for the rapid redistribution of wealth, destruction of the environment, and deporting any resource of value. This would need to be adopted by all nations south of the Brandt Line, and many north of it, particularly China and Russia. China would be wise to back off on its Westernizing, get back to basics, and find its own direction by learning from the mistakes of the West instead of adopting them.

The United States spends more than half the world's defense budget and idealistically believes itself to have moral superiority. The election of Bush by decision of the Supreme Court bought and paid for by the right exposed the move of the United States toward a fascist oligarchy and institutionalized corruption. It completely lacks any sense of responsibility or reality, acting out of desperation on one hand and uncontrolled greed on the other. Civilization cannot survive when government serves those whose world view is winning at any cost. The United States has the best government oligarch can buy without paying taxes or doing anything to help with the infrastructure or needs of the nation or population. They may have bought up the media, but reality cannot be masked for long. I am personally against any form of hostility, but reality is that desperate people resort to desperate behaviors. When the value of individual life is taken for naught, individuals will gladly sacrifice themselves to put the heads of their persecutors on pikes. This is a serious threat to civilization and the species.

The hyper-consumption of the past century, reliance on technology, and destruction of archaeological records opens civilization up not only to utter failure, but complete loss of the knowledge and resources needed to correct the ecological damage. Without the ecological damage the risk is only a dark age. With the ecological destruction and out of control population growth, the risk is extinction. Warning: population and climate change projections are almost all significantly under or miss-reported. The population doubled in less than thirty years, will double again in less than twenty, and again before mid-century. The ecosystem was already in distress when the population was half what it is today. This isn't tomorrow's problem, it is yesterday's and today's problem. Unfortunately history shows that humanity refuses to do what is right unless it is forced to. Police state fascism is not the answer, right choices are. Unfortunately violence is the language known by predatory capitalists, oligarchs, and those who serve them. History shows these individuals are masters of turning the victims on each other and away from them. This is what terrorism is really about: turning innocent victims on each other instead of directing that energy to eliminate the real problems.

Violence may be a reality, but history also shows that violent over-throws almost never turn out well or justify the sacrifices. Humans have mastered the art of destruction. Any fool can break things. If you want to be perceived as something other than wild animals, then you really need to master the arts of creation, co-existence, and respect for diversity. Those who think theirs is the only right position are a danger to everyone because they are the puppets of oligarchs. These same radicals can look to their own religious beliefs to find God creating diversity in destroying the Tower of Babel. Diversity is the way things are meant to be and is good. Society only needs fear and conflict to sustain itself so long as there are predators in the population. Hope and mutual respect build nations, religions, civilizations, and lasting power. The modern empires are dying and desperate. It is only a matter of time before they destroy themselves.

Obama is a perfect example of failed leadership and a failed state. He was elected as safe relative to the insanity of his opposition. This too is failing throughout Western Civilization. The populations are jumping between extremities. When those populations finally accept that the elections are rigged so all the candidates serve basically the same purpose, the whole system will violently implode. Populations tire of violence and eventually adopt whatever convenience will stop the violence and let them live. This is disastrous. It is bad enough to live in a thinly masked feudal state, and worse when it is overt and accepted for the sake of survival. Instead of staging a violent revolution and risking worse, let's invent a better future.

Recruiting and Training Terrorists

Introduction

This chapter closely coincides with the modis operandi. It helps us to narrow suspicious activities based on what we know without having to declassify documents. We know who does the training, who gets trained, what they are trained to do, and how the tactics were learned in the first place.

Recruiting

The idea of training programs is that those trained by Americans then take their knowledge to new recruits and train them. In this manner, the CIA manual is like a virus infesting itself within the society. Indoctrination starts small, building rapport through little things, like setting aside weapons and helping locals with their work. As rapport becomes established, propaganda increases until finally new recruits start formal training. The CIA recommends a 14-day intensive program at that point.

The recruiting strategy recommended by the CIA to the Contras of Nicaragua is extremely revealing of how common good people become involved in terrorism. The following text is from Chapter 5: Development And Control Of Front Organizations, in the CIA from the manual already extensively referenced. The scariest part of this text is that targets for recruiting are common, honest, law-abiding citizens. Pay particular attention to part 2, paragraphs 1 and 4.

1. Generalities

The development and control of front organizations (or "facade" organizations) is an essential process in the guerrilla effort to carry out the insurrection. That is, in truth, an aspect of urban guerrilla warfare, but it should advance parallel to the campaign in the rural area. This section has as its objective to give the guerrilla student an understanding of the development and control of front organizations in guerrilla warfare.

2. Initial Recruitment

The initial recruitment to the movement, if it is involuntary, will be carried out through several "private" consultations with a cadre (without his knowing that he is talking to a member of ours). Then, the recruit will be informed that he or she is already inside the movement, and he will be exposed to the police of the regime if he or she does not cooperate.

When the guerrillas carry out missions of armed propaganda and a program of regular visits to the towns by the Armed Propaganda Teams, these contacts will provide the commandos with the names and places of persons who can be recruited. The recruitment, which will be voluntary, is done through visits by guerrilla leaders or political cadres.

After a chain of voluntary recruitments has been developed, and the trustworthiness of the recruits has been established by their carrying out small missions, they will be instructed about increasing/widening the chain by recruiting in specific target groups, in accordance with the following procedure:

From among their acquaintances or through observation of the target groups - political parties, workers' unions, youth groups, agrarian associations, etc. - finding out the personal habits, preferences and biases, as well as the weaknesses of the "recruitable" individuals.

Make an approach through an acquaintance, and if possible, develop a friendship, attracting him through his preferences or weaknesses: it might be inviting him for lunch in the restaurant of his choice or having a drink in his favorite cantina or an invitation to dinner in the place he prefers.

Recruitment should follow one of the following guidelines:

- If in an informal conversation the target seems susceptible to voluntary recruitment based on his beliefs and personal values, etc., the political cadre assigned to carry out the recruitments will be notified of this. The original contact will indicate to the cadre assigned, in detail, all he knows of the prospective recruit, and the style of persuasion to be used, introducing the two.

Recruiting and Training Terrorists

- If the target does not seem to be susceptible to voluntary recruitment, meetings can be arranged which seem casual with the guerrilla leaders or with the political cadres (unknown by the target until that moment). The meetings will be held so that "other persons" know that the target is attending them, whether they see him arrive at a particular house, seated at the table in a particular bar or even seated on a park bench. The target, then, is faced with the fact of his participation in the insurrectional struggle and it will be indicated to him also that if he fails to cooperate or to carry out future orders, he will be subjected to reprisals by the police or soldiers of the regime.
- The notification of the police, denouncing a target who does not want to join the guerrillas, can be carried out easily, when it becomes necessary, through a letter with false statements of citizens who are not implicated in the movement. Care should be taken that the person who recruited him covertly is not discovered.
- With the carrying out of clandestine missions for the movement, the involvement and handing over of every recruit is done gradually on a wider and wider scale, and confidence increases. This should be a gradual process, in order to prevent confessions from fearful individuals who have been assigned very difficult or dangerous missions too early.

Using this recruitment technique, our guerrillas will be able to successfully infiltrate any key target group in the regime, in order to improve the internal control of the enemy structure.

Who Gets Trained

Conventional wisdom concerns itself with the guy who straps a bomb to his body then tries to blow up a nightclub, or who gets some compatriots together, hijacks a plane or takes a group of hostages. These are relatively minor, and typically require little or no training, except maybe what is needed to inspire participation. As we saw with 9/11, this type of terrorist may need to learn a particular skill, like flying a plane, which they acquire like everyone else does (note to see who profited, including Cheney, Bush, and the CIA, simply search the Internet for CIA investment 9/11). Common people are often the targets, as the following from the CIA manual excerpt (Chapter 4, part 2, paragraph 6) illustrates:

> The source of basic recruitment for guerrilla cadres will be the same social groups of Nicaraguans to whom the psychological campaign is directed, such as peasants, students, professionals, housewives, etc. The campesinos (peasants) should be made to see that they do not have lands; the workers that the State is putting an end to factories and industries; the doctors, that they are being replaced by Cuban paramedics, and that as doctors they cannot practice their profession due to lack of medicines. A requirement for recruiting them will be their ability to express themselves in public.

When we see consorted low-level terrorism, we observe an elite group of senior terrorists who have either been formally trained in high-level terrorism, or learned it through personal observation and study. These leaders, though the scope of their purpose is local or regional, must be looked upon as belonging to the higher category, while their followers clearly belong to the lower. It is said that one man's terrorist is another's freedom fighter. In essence, these low-level terrorists without a state, are desperate individuals who do not see another alternative to expelling a government they oppose. Their targets are typically local. There are, of course, many instances of these groups reaching outside their geographic centers of operations. Examples include bombings of embassies, the attacks on the World Trade Center, hijackings, etc. These are clearly directed to bring outside attention to the local issues.

High-level international terrorism tends to act over a region, particularly a nation, over an extended period of time. It is a long-term psychological war for power. What else differentiates high-level from low-level terrorism is the selfishness. Low-level terrorism tends to be more selfless, seeking to right a perceived wrong. As such, low-level terrorism has an inexhaustible recruit base. High-level terrorism, on the other hand, assigns, increases, or maintains the power of the elite. Power is being inflicted against the will of the masses. This requires careful training in the fine arts of psychological warfare.

In order to address the question of who gets trained for high-level terrorism, we must distinguish between levels of participation. First, you have the highest group, the potential dictators or controlling elite. Below these you have their tacticians, field commanders, operatives, and "foot soldiers."

Dictators and the ruling elite are selected based upon greed. Those who desire power and/or wealth, or otherwise oppose the regime to be toppled and are soft toward American interests are a popular choice. They must already be in a leadership role with adherents, from whom are drawn the other trainees. At this level of terrorism, triggermen do not need to be radicals; they need only be willing to carry out orders.

The following text, again from Chapters 1 and 5 of the CIA manual specify potential candidates for recruiting. Paragraph 2 of 1.5 and paragraph 1 of 5.3 deserve particular attention.

1.5. Development and Control of the "Front" Organizations

The development and control of "front" (or facade) organizations is carried out through subjective internal control at group meetings of "inside cadres," and the calculations of the time for the fusion of these combined efforts to be applied to the masses.

Established citizens-doctors, lawyers, businessmen, teachers, etc.- will be recruited initially as "Social Crusaders" in typically "innocuous" movements in the area of operations. When their "involvement" with the clandestine organization is revealed to them, this supplies the psychological pressure to use them as "inside cadres" in groups to which they already belong or of which they can be members.

Then they will receive instruction in techniques of persuasion over control of target groups to support our democratic revolution, through a gradual and skillful process. A cell control system isolates individuals from one another, and at the appropriate moment, their influence is used for the fusion of groups in a united national front.

5.3. Established Citizens, Subjective Internal Control

Established citizens, such as doctors, lawyers, businessmen, landholders, minor state officials, etc., will be recruited to the movement and used for subjective internal control of groups and associations to which they belong or may belong.

Once the recruitment/involvement has been brought about, and has progressed to the point that allows that specific instructions be given to internal cadres to begin to influence their groups, instructions will be given to them to carry out the following:

- The process is simple and only requires a basic knowledge of the Socrates dialectic: that is the knowledge that is inherent to another person or the established position of a group, some theme, some word or some thought related to the objective of persuasion of the person in charge of our recruitment.

- The cadre then must emphasize this theme, word or thought in the discussions or meetings of the target group, through a casual commentary, which improves the focus of other members of the group in relation to this. Specific examples are:

Economic interest groups are motivated by profit and generally feel that the system hinders the use of their capability in this effort in some way, taxes, import-export tariffs, transportation costs, etc. The cadre in charge will increase this feeling of frustration in later conversations.

Political aspirants, particularly if the are not successful, feel that the system discriminates against them unfairly, limiting their capabilities, because the Sandinista regime does not allow elections. The cadres should focus political discussions towards this frustration.

Recruiting and Training Terrorists

Intellectual social critics (such as professors, teachers, priests, missionaries, etc.), generally feel that the government ignores their valid criticism or censors their comments unjustly, especially in a situation of revolution. This can easily be shown by the guerrilla cadre at meetings and discussions, to be an injustice of the system.

For all the target groups, after they have established frustrations, the hostility towards the obstacles to their aspirations will gradually become transferred to the current regime and its system of repression.

The guerrilla cadre moving among the target groups should always maintain a low profile, so that the development of hostile feelings towards the false Sandinista regime seems to come spontaneously from the members of the group and not from suggestions of the cadres. This is internal subjective control.

Anti-governmental hostility should be generalized, and not necessarily in our favor. If a group develops a feeling in our favor, it can be utilized. But the main objective is to precondition the target groups for the fusion in mass organizations later in the operation, when other activities have been successfully undertaken.

Training Centers

Daniel Ellsberg made a very strong case for the behavior of Federal employees. He notes that if you work for the Executive Branch, you often get a feeling of being above or beyond the law. The belief is that if you are commanded to do a thing, then it must be legal. Even if you know that it is illegal, then the fact that you are ordered to do so implies that there is an exception, like police running red lights, breaking the speed limit, or discharging a firearm in public. If you are ordered to burn down a village, you do it. If you are ordered to drop bombs on a target, you are not given the opportunity to see who you are dropping the bombs on, and no alternative short of Levinworth for insubordination. In essence, this structure makes good, law-abiding citizens, terrorists, and all military facilities, particularly boot camps, terrorist training centers.

The widely known "training center for terrorists" in the US is the School of the Americas (SOA), renamed the "Western Hemisphere Institute for Security Cooperation" (WHISC) in January 2001. The SOA was founded in 1946, and originally operated in Panama. It was later moved to Fort Benning, Georgia. It has the acclaim of graduating some 60,000 Latin American "soldiers" and "policemen" between 1946 and 2001. I must note that upon comparing graduation rates with regime changes, it appears that the SOA is a school for subject states and not for revolutionaries. It appears, not only from this but also in the documentation of the coups and other regime changes, that revolutionaries are trained by "advisors" and not at Fort Benning. On the other hand, many of SOA's graduates are directly linked to terror of new regimes. The curve for graduates from a country typically explodes immediately following a regime change favoring the US, as does the increase in psychological warfare and atrocities committed by the new regimes against their own people.

While an argument could be posed for widespread de facto terrorist training throughout the Executive Branch, WHISC goes beyond any doubt. Federal employees must take the route of Ellsberg. Refuse to participate, stand up and expose the atrocities or be counted among the perpetrators. According to Federal law and the statements of various presidents, including George W. Bush, this is the right thing to do. Otherwise the perpetrators willing to violate the laws of the land are themselves enemies of the American people and the people of the world. As Benjamin Franklin once said, alluding to the tyranny of King George, "Aristotle calls all princes tyrants, from the moment they set up an interest different from that of their subjects."

Curriculum

Pouring through the record of known graduates, most of the courses appear innocuous enough, such as standard military training courses, mechanics, engineering, field medical services, and even cooking. A few items that slip through though raised my eyebrows and will raise yours also, such as Nuclear Warfare (also Especial de Guerra Nuclear), military intelligence interrogation, counterinsurrection (contrainsurrección), counterinsurgency, counter resistance, and psychological operations (operaciones sicologicas). I observe that obvious titles like mass murder do not appear on the list. This is either because it is not taught at the SOA, the information is incomplete, or the information is misleading. The fact is, somewhere, somehow, the US does train for mass murder, and I would not be surprised if some of the eyebrow raisers above are where such is taught.

What exactly do you teach people about mass murder? The US and USSR had the "fortune" of getting the scoop on this from the greatest masters of mass murder in history: the Nazis and the Japanese. Since they took their lessons from there, let us look at the qualities and necessities of mass murder that does what it was meant to.

The Germans, like the Japanese, started with terrorizing the population with senseless beating, killings, and rapes. Eventually they found themselves overwhelmed with "undesirables" and started killing them by the thousands and dumping the bodies in mass graves. The "Final Solution" was created because Heinrich Himler inspected his Einsatzgruppen after they had murdered over a million Jews in Eastern Europe the hard way: one bullet at a time. His orders were to find a method that would not be so demoralizing on his troops. Apparently they had forgotten about the German Western front during the Great War, when German soldiers were so nauseated by the mindless slaughter that many stopped shooting. Anyway, the next simpler solution was hermetically sealed vans, with the exhaust fed into the back. They would load Jews, homosexuals, and gypsies in the backs of the vans then simply drive around. This was still quite messy, because they still had to clean out the trucks and dispose of the bodies. The death camps made the whole situation quite industrial. The killers really did not have to look at the bodies, as able-bodied prisoners had the job of removing the bodies and destroying them in the ovens. The killers needed only to lead the victims into the gas chambers and then supervise everything else from there. We should further note that the death camps were almost exclusively in Poland, so German citizens would not accidentally see them.

The Japanese had a completely different model to build upon, some of which US forces have adopted and used. The Japanese took out their aggression on Chinese, and the logic of their aggression was simple. They sought to terrorize the Chinese into cooperation and subjugation. To do this they destroyed villages, they maimed, raped, murdered and dismembered without regard for age. They Japanese soldiers were convinced the Chinese were monsters. One said that when they raped a Chinese girl, they thought of her as a woman. But when they were done raping her, she became and object and a monster, therefore disposable.

We learn much from these atrocities. First, atrocities are a means to instill fear (in our last chapter we will discuss the concept of fear is power). Second, to commit the atrocities you must have a system to do so. If you have people committing murder face-to-face, you must rotate out the murderers before they become affected by the killing. Also, the murderers must be psychologically primed to believe that they are not killing humans. Ideally, the best way to commit mass murder is at a distance and impersonally. A bomber has an easier time dropping a bomb blindly that results in the deaths of forty people than a gunner having to shoot each one in person. The US uses this to its extremity with long-range weapons and the use of other forces for in-person combat and murder. We should also note that in Iraq, the US used bulldozers to bury the enemy alive, which is also impersonal.

Recruiting and Training Terrorists

Bodies in the street deliver a strong message to the people in the area, and were common in both Asia and Europe during WWII. Heads on pikes, dismembered bodies, impaled bodies, and bodies floating down the river or washing up on shore were popular for the Japanese. They have certainly had their periods of popularity in European history. The horror of mutilated bodies delivers a very harsh message and assures no voice of opposition. Disappearances are not quite as effective, but do create fear. Therefore, what we often see with disappearances is that some of the bodies later wash up on the shore dismembered, implying that all those who disappear are tortured and murdered.

Throughout the text we will regularly reference the CIA's manual entitled Psychological Operations. This is apparently an official document used for training Nicaraguan Contras. It was written in Spanish and translated by an undisclosed person and openly distributed in the US. The manual is intended for teaching revolutionaries, not training dictators. That helps to explain why the SOA graduation records and escalation in atrocities appear to occur after the major events, rather than before.

Group Dynamics

Chapter 2 of the CIA manual emphasizes training and a group structure. It also points out the value of keeping the rebels miserable so they are encouraged to continue their rebellion against the source of the misery, which is of course the existing government. Chapter 4 then continues this with explaining how the nuclei are formed. Chapter 5 deals with front organizations, and specifies three persons, which is exactly what the NVA and Viet Cong used in Vietnam against the US and France: groups of three who can easily watch after each other and blatant openness and frank honesty among members (Davidson, 1991, p. 63). Pay close attention to the last two paragraphs of 2.3, paragraphs 3 and 8 of 4.4, and "Our key agitators should avoid places of disturbances, once they have taken care of the beginning of the same" in part 4.5.

2.2. Political Awareness

The individual political awareness of the guerrilla, the reason for his struggle, will be as important as his ability in combat. This political awareness and motivation will be achieved:

- By improving the combat potential of the guerrilla by improving his motivation for fighting.

- By the guerrilla recognizing himself as a vital tie between the democratic guerrillas and the people, whose support is essential for the subsistence of both.

- By fostering the support of the population for the national insurgence through the support for the guerrillas of the locale, which provides a psychological basis in the population for politics after the victory has been achieved.

- By developing trust in the guerrillas and in the population, for the reconstruction of a local and national government.

- By promoting the value of participation by the guerrillas and the people in the civic affairs of the insurrection and in the national programs.

- By developing in each guerrilla the ability of persuasion face- to-face, at the local level, to win the support of the population, which is essential for success in guerrilla warfare.

2.3. Group Dynamics

This political awareness building and motivation are attained by the use of group dynamics at the level of small units. The group discussion method and self-criticism are a general guerrilla training and operations technique.

Group discussions raise the spirit and increase the unity of thought in small guerrilla groups and exercise social pressure on the weakest members to better carry out their mission in training and future combat actions. These group discussions will give special emphasis to:

Recruiting and Training Terrorists

- Creating a favorable opinion of our movement. Through local and national history, make it clear that the Sandinista regime is "foreignizing," "repressive" and "imperialistic," and that even though there are some Nicaraguans within the government, point out that they are "puppets" of the power of the Soviets and Cubans, i.e. of foreign power.

- Always a local focus. Matters of an international nature will be explained only in support of local events in the guerrilla warfare.

- The unification of the nation is our goal. This means that the defeat of the Sandinista armed forces is our priority. Our insurrectional movement is a pluralistic political platform from which we are determined to win freedom, equality, a better economy with work facilities, a higher standard of living, a true democracy for all Nicaraguans without exception.

- Providing to each guerrilla clear understanding about the struggle for national sovereignty against Soviet-Cuban imperialism. Discussion guides will lead the guerrillas so that they will see the injustices of the Sandinista system.

- Showing each guerrilla the need for good behavior to win the support of the population. Discussion guides should convince the guerrillas that the attitude and opinion of the population play a decisive role, because victory is impossible without popular support.

- Self-criticism will be in constructive terms that will contribute to the mission of the movement, and which will provide the guerrillas with the conviction that they have a constant and positive individual responsibility in the mission of the group.

The method of instruction will be:

a) division of the guerrilla force into squads for group discussions, including command and support elements, whenever the tactical situation permits it. The makeup of the small units should be maintained when these groups are designated.

b) Assignment of a political cadre in the guerrilla force to each group to guide the discussion. The squad leader should help the cadre to foster study and the expression of thoughts. If there are not enough political cadres for each squad or post, leaders should guide the discussions, and the available cadres visit alternate groups.

c) It is appropriate for the cadre (or the leader) to guide the discussion of a group to cover a number of points and to reach a correct conclusion. The guerrillas should feel that it was their free and own decision. The cadre should serve as a private teacher. The cadre or leader will not act as a lecturer, but will help the members of the group to study and express their own opinions.

d) The political cadre will at the end of every discussion make a summary of the principal points, leading them to the correct conclusions. Any serious difference with the objectives of the movement should be noted by the cadre and reported to the comandante of the force. If necessary, a combined group meeting will be held and the team of political cadres will explain and rectify the misunderstanding.

e) Democratic conduct by the political cadres: living, eating and working with the guerrillas, and if possible, fighting at their side, sharing their living conditions. All of this will foster understanding and the spirit of cooperation that will help in the discussion and exchange of ideas.

f) Carry out group discussions in towns, and areas of operations whenever possible with the civilian population, and not limit them to camps or bases. This is done to emphasize the revolutionary nature of the struggle and to demonstrate that the guerrillas identified with the objectives of the people move about within the population. The guerrilla projects himself toward the people, as the political cadre does toward the guerrilla, and they should live, eat and work together to realize a unity of revolutionary thought.

The principles for guerrilla and political-cadre group discussions are:

Recruiting and Training Terrorists

- Organize discussion groups at the post or squad level. A cadre cannot be sure of the comprehension and acceptance of the concepts and conclusions by guerrillas in large groups. In a group of the size of a squad of 10 men, the judgment and control of the situation is greater. In this way, all students will participate in an exchange among them; the political leader, the group leader, and also the political cadre. Special attention will be given to the individual ability to discuss the objectives of the insurrectional struggle. Whenever a guerrilla expresses his opinion, he will be interested in listening to the opinions of others, leading as a result to the unity of thought.
- Combine the different points of view and reach an opinion or common conclusion. This is the most difficult task of a political guerrilla cadre. After the group discussions of the democratic objectives of the movement, the chief of the team of political cadres of the guerrilla force should combine the conclusions of individual groups in a general summary. At a meeting with all the discussion groups, the cadre shall provide the principal points, and the guerrillas will have the opportunity to clarify or modify their points of view. To carry this out, the conclusions will be summarized in the form of slogans, wherever possible.
- Face with honesty the national and local problems of our struggle. The political cadres should always be prepared to discuss solutions to the problems observed by the guerrillas. During the discussions, the guerrillas should be guided by the following three principles:
- Freedom of thought.
- Freedom of expression.
- Concentration of thoughts on the objectives of the democratic struggle.

The result desired is a guerrilla who in a persuasive manner can justify all of his acts whenever he is in contact with any member of the town/people, and especially with himself and with his guerrilla companions by facing the vicissitudes of guerrilla warfare.

This means that every guerrilla will come to have effective face-to- face persuasion as a combatant-propagandist in his contact with the people, to the point of giving 5-10 logical reasons why, e.g. a peasant should give him a piece of cloth, or a needle and thread to mend his clothes. When behaves in this manner, no type of propaganda of the enemy will be able to make a "terrorist" of him in the eyes of the people.

In addition, hunger, cold, fatigue and insecurity in the existence of the guerrilla acquire meaning in the cause of the struggle due to the constant psychological orientation.

4.4. Creation of Nuclei

This involves the mobilization of a specific number of agitators of the guerrilla organization of the place. This group will inevitably attract an equal number of curious persons who seek adventures and emotions, as well as those unhappy with the system of government. The guerrillas will attract sympathizers, discontented citizens as a consequence of the repression of the system. Each guerrilla subunit will be assigned specific tasks and missions that they should carry out.

Our cadres will be mobilized in the largest number possible, together with persons who have been affected by the Communist dictatorship, whether their possessions have been stolen from them, they have been incarcerated, or tortured, or suffered from any other type of aggression against them. They will be mobilized toward the areas where the hostile and criminal elements of the FSLN, CDS and others live, with an effort for them to be armed with clubs, iron rods, placards and if possible, small firearms, which they will carry hidden.

If possible, professional criminals will be hired to carry out specific selected "jobs."

Our agitators will visit the places where the unemployed meet, as well as the unemployment offices, in order to hire them for unspecified "jobs." The recruitment of these wage earners is necessary because a nucleus is created under absolute orders.

Recruiting and Training Terrorists

The designated cadres will arrange ahead of time the transportation of the participants, in order to take them to meeting places in private or public vehicles, boats or any other type of transportation.

Other cadres will be designated to design placards, flags and banners with different slogans or key words, whether they be partial, temporary or of the most radical type.

Other cadres will be designated to prepare flyers, posters, signs and pamphlets to make the concentration more noticeable. This material will contain instructions for the participants and will also serve against the regime.

Specific tasks will be assigned to others, in order to create a "martyr" for the cause, taking the demonstrators to a confrontation with the authorities, in order to bring about uprisings or shootings, which will cause the death of one or more persons, who would become the martyrs, a situation that should be made use of immediately against the regime, in order to create greater conflicts.

4.5. Ways to Lead an Uprising at Mass Meetings

It can be carried out by means of a small group of guerrillas infiltrated within the masses, who will have the mission of agitating, giving the impression that there are many of them and that they have popular backing. Using the tactics of a force of 200-300 agitators, a demonstration can be created in which 1,000-2,000 persons take part.

The agitation of the masses in a demonstration is carried out by means of sociopolitical objectives. In this action one or several people of our convert movement should take part, highly trained as mass agitators, involving innocent persons, in order to bring about an apparent spontaneous protest demonstration. They will lead all of the concentration to the end of it.

Outside Commando. This element stays out of all activity, located so that they can observe from where they are the development of the planned events. As a point of observation, they should look for the tower of a church, a high building, a high tree, the highest level of the stadium or an auditorium, or any other high place.

Inside Commando. This element will remain within the multitude. Great importance should be given to the protection of the leaders of these elements. Some placards or large allusive signs should be used to designate the Commando Posts and to provide signals to the subunits. This element will avoid placing itself in places where fights or incidents come about after the beginning of the demonstration.

These key agitators of ours will remain within the multitude. The one responsible for this mission will assign ahead of time the agitators to remain near the placard that he will indicate to them, in order to give protection to the placard from any contrary element. In that way the commander will know where our agitators are, and will be able to send orders to change passwords or slogans, or any other unforeseen thing, and even eventually to incite violence if he desires it.

At this stage, once the key cadres have been dispersed, they should place themselves in visible places such as by signs, lampposts, and other places which stand out.

Our key agitators should avoid places of disturbances, once they have taken care of the beginning of the same.

Defense Posts. These elements will act as bodyguards in movement, forming a ring of protection for the chief, protecting him from the police and the army, or helping him to escape if it should be necessary. They should be highly disciplined and will react only upon a verbal order from the chief.

In case the chief participates in a religious concentration, a funeral or any other type of activity in which they have to behave in an organized fashion, the bodyguards will remain in the ranks very close to the chief or to the placard or banner carriers in order to give them full protection.

The participants in this mission should be guerrilla combatants in civilian clothes, or hired recruits who are sympathizers in our struggle and who are against the oppressive regime.

Recruiting and Training Terrorists

These members must have a high discipline and will use violence only on the verbal orders of the one in charge of them.

Messengers. They should remain near the leaders, transmitting orders between the inside and outside commandos. They will use communication radios, telephones, bicycles, motorcycles, cars, or move on foot or horseback, taking paths or trails to shorten distances. Adolescents (male and female) are ideal for this mission.

Shock Troops. These men should be equipped with weapons (Knives, razors, chains, clubs, bludgeons) and should march slightly behind the innocent and gullible participants. They should carry their weapons hidden. They will enter into action only as "reinforcements" if the guerrilla agitators are attacked by the police. They will enter the scene quickly, violently and by surprise, in order to distract the authorities, in this way making possible the withdrawal or rapid escape of the inside commando.

Carriers of Banners and Placards. The banners and placards used in demonstrations or concentrations will express the protests of the population, but when the concentration reaches its highest level of euphoria or popular discontent, our infiltrated persons will make use of the placards against the regime, which we manage to infiltrate in a hidden fashion, an don them slogans or key words will be expressed to the benefit of our cause. The one responsible for this mission will assign the agitators ahead of time to keep near the placard of any contrary element. In that way, the comandante will know where the agitators are, and will be able to send orders to change slogans and eventually to incite violence if he wishes.

Agitators of Rallying Cries and Applause. They will be trained with specific instructions to use tried rallying cries. They will be able to use phrase such as "WE ARE HUNGRY, WE WANT BREAD," and "WE DON'T WANT COMMUNISM." There work and their technique for agitating the masses is quite similar to those of the leaders of applause and slogans at the high school football or baseball games. The objective is to become more adept and not just to shout rallying cries.

5.4. Organizations of Cells for Security

Internal cadres of our movement should organize into cells of three persons, only one of them maintaining outside contact.

The cell of three persons is the basic element of the movement, with frequent meetings to receive orders and pass information to the cell leader. These meetings are also very important for mutually reinforcing the members of the cell, as well as their morale. They should exercise criticism of themselves on the realization or failures in carrying out individual subjective control missions.

The coordination of the three-member cell provides a security net for reciprocal communication, each member having contact with only an operational cell. The members will not reveal at the cell coordination meetings the identity of their contact in an operational cell; they will reveal only the nature of the activity in which the cell is involved, e.g., political party work, medical association work, etc.

There is no hierarchy in cells outside of an element of coordination, who is the leader, who will have direct but covert contact with our guerrilla comandante in the zone or operational area. The previous diagram does not indicate which new operational cell is the limit, but it indicates that for every three operational cells, we need a coordination cell.

Graduate Record

Unfortunately, since the SOA has been the main focus of most research, little is known of those who went to other schools in significantly smaller numbers (or more greatly dispersed). The pie chart is based on the 38,198 graduates listed by the School of the Americas Watch (http://www.soaw.org). This number is interesting for two reasons. First, it does not account for about 22,000 graduates. The data has other problems also. For example, SOA (WHISC or as DOD calls it, WHINSEC) is only

Recruiting and Training Terrorists

one training center. Frankly, SOA has received so much attention, they have been whitewashed and now have their own website (http://www.benning.army.mil/whinsec), stage "tours", etc. Very likely the real operation has moved on.

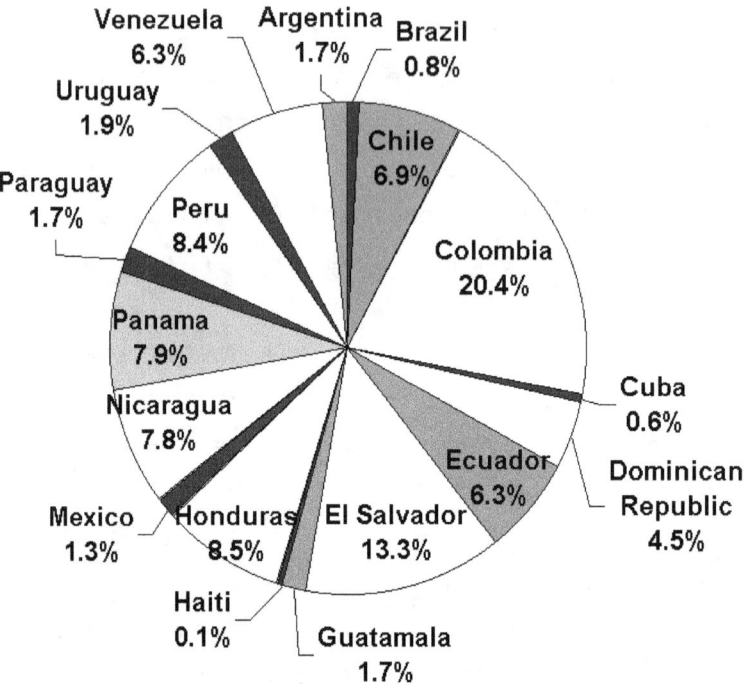

Some sources mention Fort Bragg, others mention Texas, which is drastically generic. Clearly the US government doesn't want the general population knowing about terrorist training. In fact, SOA had remained in Panama until 1984, and became radically exposed in 1996 when seven manuals were released exposing its very politically incorrect curriculum. The table below identifies the six that were seen as having materials inconsistent with US policy and American values (the seventh was Analysis I, 60 pages). A discussion of objectionable materials appears at http://www.gwu.edu/~nsarchiv/nsa/archive/news/ dodmans.htm.

Spanish Title	English	Pages
Manejo de Fuente	Handling Resources*	174
Contrainteligencia	Counterintelligence*	310
Terrorismo y Guerrilla Urbana	Terrorism and the Urban Guerrilla	175
Interrogacion	Interrogation	150
Inteligencia de Combate	Combat Intelligence	172
Guerra Revolucionaria y Ideologia Comunista	Revolutionary War and Communist Ideology	128

These manuals were used by Mobile Training Teams (1987-89) and by the SOA (1989-91). A full discussion of these with sample text is at http://www.lawg.org/manuals.htm. The manuals were written in Spanish only, with no English translations prepared. The first two listings are available in English. The first three listings are available at http://www.soaw.org/new/article.php?id=98. Spanish versions of all but the last manual are available through http://www.derechos.org/nizkor/la/ (Counterintelligence is at http://www.derechos.net/soaw/manuals/ci-toc.html). I have not found a web version of the last manual. You can use an online resource, like AltaVista's translation utility to help interpret these. Supposedly these manuals were not approved by the proper command. Perhaps I'm too cynical, or maybe I've seen too much inside information on similar matters, but I don't believe it for a moment. Frankly, based on Ellsberg's experiences, Reagan knew and approved of these, and Bush very likely knew of them also. They are simply too sensitive, and somehow their authorship is never mentioned at all. Did they pass through regular channels? No. Three CIA manuals also leaked, one of which is referenced numerously in this text, one that was used in Vietnam, and the Freedom Fighter's Manual (full text at http://www.cnn.com/SPECIALS/cold.war/ episodes/18/documents/cia.contra/index.html). Again, no mention of authorship, etc.

While many graduates are definitely associated with atrocities, we should note the atrocities do not typically occur during a revolution by the US-sponsored revolutionary force, which is explained by the CIA manual already cited. A relationship exists between historical events (e.g. coups, mass murders, etc.) and peaks in graduation. Furthermore, countries with long track records of atrocities consistently have large numbers of SOA graduates. On each graph is a note identifying US or CIA involvement (7 coups, 1 revolt, 1 assassination, and 1 intervention in 9 countries). Nixon's "War on Drugs" is put on Colombia's chart. Graduation for Colombians then peaks each time the US needs a good distraction and to focus on drug trade (e.g. 1976 covers up NVA taking over South Vietnam, 1980 was good for the election but not good enough, 1983 and beyond serve too many purposes to list here). Colombia is said to have the worst track record of atrocities in Latin America (and continues). It also has the greatest number of SOA grads.

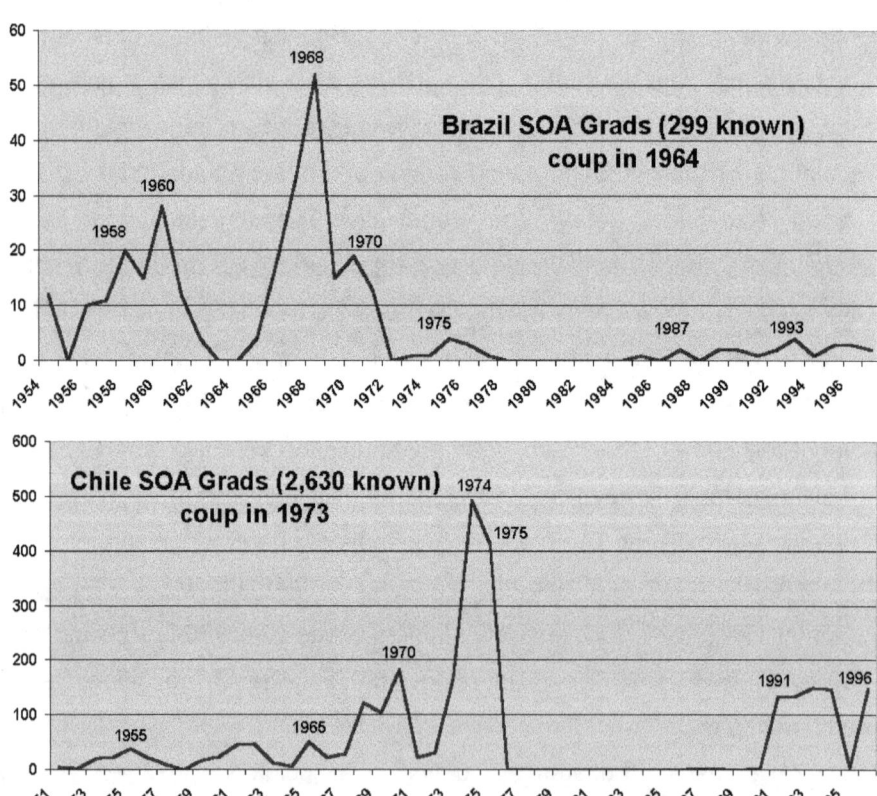

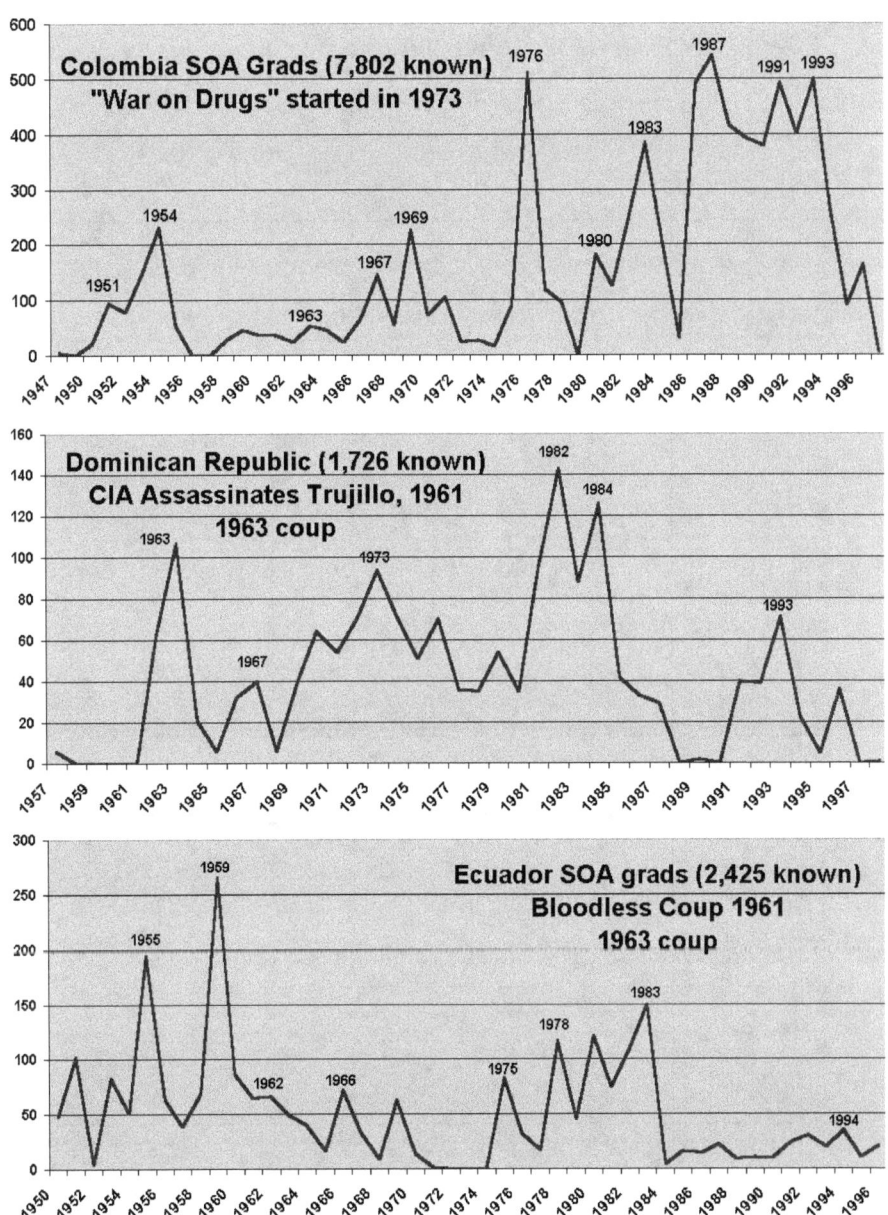

Recruiting and Training Terrorists

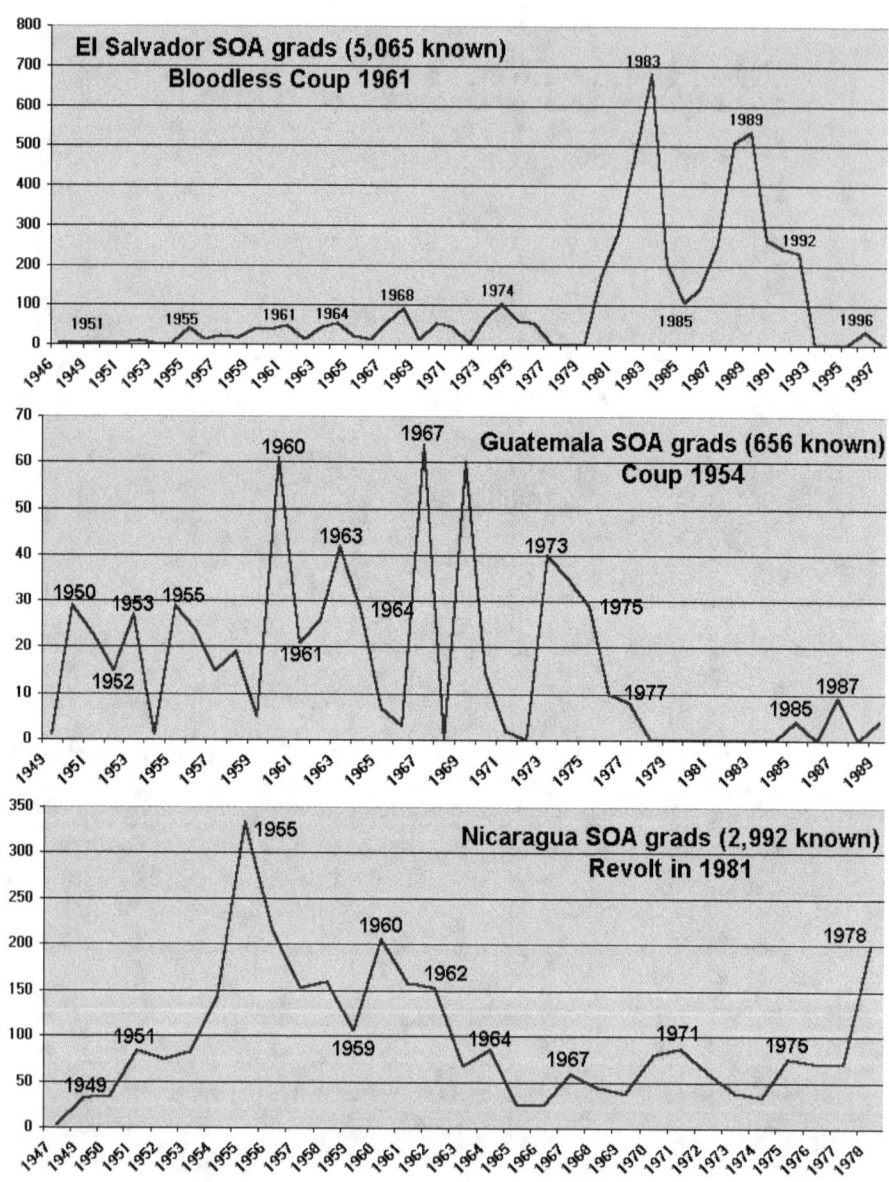

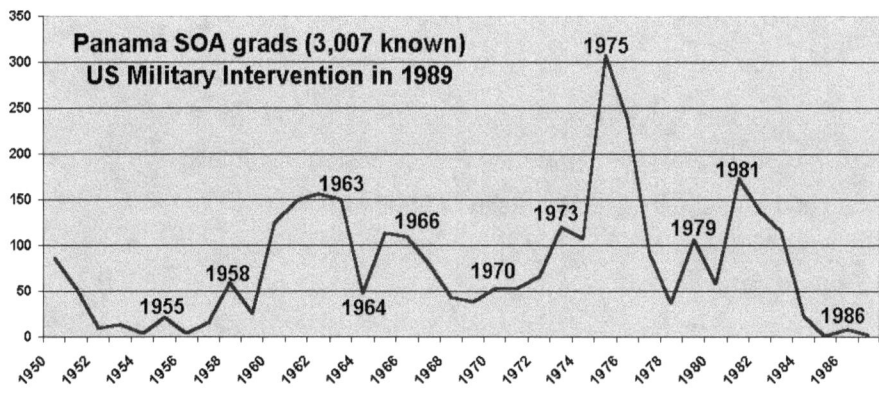

The following list gives you a brief idea of the track records of SOA graduates.

- Robert D'Aubuisson, death squad leader, El Salvador, who murdered Jesuit priests in 1989

- Byron Lima Estrada, convicted in Guatemala City of murdering Bishop Juan Gerardi in 1998. Estrada ran D-2 with two other grads, which destroyed 448 Mayan villages

- Roberto Viola and Leopold Galtieri, Argentine dictators

- Manuel Noriega and Omar Torrijos, Panamanian dictators

- Juan Velsaco Alvarado, Peruvian dictator

- Guillermo Rodriguez, Ecuadorian dictator

- The commander responsible for the 1994 Ocosingo massacre in Mexico

- 19 of the 26 soldiers of D'Aubuisson's death squads.

- Augusto Pinochet's 3 concentration camps run by graduates

- 4 of the 5 officers commanding the Honduran death squad of the 1980's, Battalion 3-16

- US State Department reported two graduates as the murderers of Alex Lopera.

- Graduates are now involved in Colombia, with US support

Recruiting and Training Terrorists

- Human Rights Watch identified seven graduates now running paramilitary groups in Colombia, responsible for commissioned kidnappings, disappearances, murders, and massacres.
- February 2001, one graduate was convicted of complicity in the torture and killing of thirty peasants in Colombia.

Conclusion

The CIA manual has the fingerprints of history all over it. The track record listed above does not look good for the graduates of the SOA. Too bad we don't know enough about other operations to be more informative, as the SOA appears to be implemented more after the fact than before, and most of the known curriculum is relatively harmless. The evidence, however, shows that the training is anything but harmless, as these individuals wreak havoc and terror on their communities to support their regimes.

Orwellian Hell

Introduction

George Orwell is the pen name for one Eric Blare (1903 - 1950; died of tuberculosis). Since he is best known by his pen name, we will continue to use it. Orwell was a journalist, "democratic socialist", mercenary, and ultimately wrote a number of books critical of journalism, official history, totalitarianism, and public oppression. He was a political cynic and a devout anti-utopian. Ironically, his anti-utopian quality was in direct opposition to his being a socialist as we tend to see the term. He wrote numerous articles, most famous of which was "Politics and the English Language." Frankly, if you want into his head, read all his essays. He wrote extensively on the Spanish Civil War, in which he participated. His most famous writings were among his last: "Animal Farm" and "1984". Both of these political satires are dark, anti-utopian stories with strong realistic themes. While "Animal Farm" is far fetched with respect to the characters, the story illustrates a revolution lead by idealism that ultimately leads to totalitarian oppression, and regenerates the popular revolution in the working class.

"1984" on the other hand, from 1948, is excessively graphic to the extent that no one could believe it. Many, in fact, thought the date was literal, and breathed sighs of relief when 1984 came around and the story did not appear to be true. Little did these people realize how much of Orwell's world had become real, even during his lifetime. The biggest difference between Orwell's Oceania and Western Civilization in 1984 (and today) was (and is) the efficiency. In terms of Big Brother, Western Civilization has a foothold, but nowhere near the stranglehold of Oceania, though we occasionally try. If anything, Western Civilization has learned how to have the stranglehold without being obvious. Technology has certainly aided the oppression of individuals, but is still too costly and inefficient to be as effective. We are also fortunate to have the Red Scare half a century behind us, though new witch-hunts are always added. We certainly have our "Ministry of Truth" cloaked under the guise of several other names, most of which culminate in the White House (perfected by Nixon's administration, I might add).

Orwell successfully showed that fear is power in most extraordinary ways, but forgot to state it among his fundamental truths of Oceania. These fundamental truths also pertain directly to our world situation throughout the Cold War and up to present. Most of us are familiar with these: War is Peace, Freedom is Slavery, Ignorance is Strength (with 2 + 2 = 5). In the following sections we will examine these truths individually, how they appertain to our situation in dealing with our social struggles including terrorism, and how we can overcome them.

Fear is Power

> (H)igh sentiments always win in the end, leaders who offer blood, toil, tears and sweat always get more out of their followers than those who offer safety and a good time.
>
> Orwell, "The Art of Donald McGill," p. 114 of A Collection of Essays

In Orwell's hell, the state of Oceania has three potential sources of fear: Big Brother and the secret police, Goldstein and his rebels, and the current foreign foe of the perpetual war. Goldstein and his rebels, and the war are both sources of power for the party of Big Brother. For those who fear Big Brother, they can find solace in Goldstein, who is most likely an illusion constructed by the inner party. For those who fear neither Goldstein nor Big Brother, they fear the bombs of enemy states. In the end, everyone has at least one fear of these three, and everyone has their own unique fear that they could be exposed to in room 101. Room 101 is Big Brother's ultimate weapon. Those who dare to not fear Big Brother, Goldstein, or the war, are taught in room 101 to fear and to surrender their sense of identity to that fear. In surrendering their identity, they give Big Brother the power he desires. Should this not succeed, then the individual is executed publicly to encourage the fear in the masses. Either way, Big Brother wins and the individual loses.

The fear of Oceania's population keeps them in control, and helps justify the oppression they live under. The same is true throughout history in all cultures. Fear of starvation led to the empowerment of Hitler. Fear of Hitler led to the empowerment of Churchill. Fear of crime led to gun control. Fear of drugs led to the drug war, and further enhanced US covert operations and terrorism. Fear of terrorism led to the enactment of the Patriot Act. Fear gives George W. Bush the power he wants to wage his war and threaten to take away yet more civil rights. This is a vicious cycle.

The idea of an Orwellian hell is dark. It is a hell raised from the ashes of revolution, built on the shoulders of workers, and sustained by fear. It is the blood of the common person who gets spilled for the sake of the perpetual war waged solely for the sake of keeping fear levels high, which in turn makes governments powerful. Orwell recognized this at least three times in his writing. In the following passage from "Looking Back on the Spanish War" (Chapter V) he lays out the framework, which foreshadows the perpetual struggle themes of both Animal Farm and 1984.

To the British working class the massacre of their comrades in Vienna, Berlin, Madrid, or wherever it might be seemed less interesting and less important than yesterday's football match. Yet this does not alter the fact that the working class will go on struggling against fascism after the others have caved in. One feature of the Nazi conquest of France was the astonishing defections among the intelligentsia, including some of the left-wing political intelligentsia. The intelligentsia are the people who squeal loudest about fascism, and yet a respectable proportion of the collapse into defeatism when the pinch comes. They are far-sighted enough to see the odds against them, and moreover they can be bribed…. With the working class it is the other way about. Too ignorant to see through the trick that is being played on them, they easily swallow the promises of fascism, yet sooner or later they always take up the struggle again. They must do so, because in their own bodies they always discover that the promises of fascism cannot be fulfilled. To win over the working class permanently, the fascists would have to raise the general standard of living, which they are unable and probably unwilling to do. The struggle of the working class is like the growth of a plant. The plant is blind and stupid, but it knows enough to keep pushing upwards toward the light, and it will do this in the face of endless discouragements.

The idea of the Orwellian hell is an idealistic utopia. In this utopia, all people are created equally within virtual castes, which is basically fascism. We must acknowledge that the ultimate form of communism is also the greatest extremity of democracy. It is democracy taken beyond the bounds of human capability. The United States is not a democracy, though it pretends to be, and the people are fooled into believing it. The true nature of the United States is a form of fascist capitalism. Ironically, capitalism seems most fitting the human condition, namely the normal human urges for personal growth, enrichment, and motivation. Perfect communism also comes close to a form of anarchy. This is not a state of lawlessness, but rather a state in which people are self-controlling. H.G. Wells wrote of such a society, driven by Maslow's self-actualization needs, in his Men Like Gods. The common people thrown into this perfect system became an infection, trying to take advantage of the self-lessness of the people. Their greed ultimately destroys them, as the people of the perfect world realize the threat and simply eliminate it as a last resort. At least one character survives to tell the story, only because he had not followed the paths of his compatriots.

I cannot pretend to have all the answers, no one does. One thing stands out among all anti-utopian authors: there is no functional utopia. People are simply different; therefore a utopia is not possible. This, however, has not stopped governments and leaders from attempting to build utopias. The Twentieth Century proved that such efforts result in totalitarianism, and ultimately the overthrow of the regime. Capitalism is gradually taking over the world, and seems inescapable. Since it seems realistically ideal for the human condition, there is no reason to suggest averting it. We do, however, need to recognize its dangers, as it is closely related to ideas that are catastrophic. Unfortunately, while I say the United States is driven by capitalism, it is driven by a shortsighted form, which demands immediate gratification. The consequence is that the United States is twisting this idea into a platform of oppression, which must be stopped by educating the people.

FDR once said, "The only thing we have to fear is fear itself." I tend to agree, but only in part. What then should scare you? Ignorance of the population leading to their fear, and/or desperation of the population should instill fear in you, because both lead to infringement on your rights, and regimes that tend toward atrocities.

All of this is of course buried under the guise of righteousness and applied at the lowest, most ignorant levels of society. Consider the following three telling statements:

The only propaganda line open to the Nazis and Fascists was to present themselves as Christian patriots saving Spain from a Russian dictatorship. This involved pretending that life in Government Spain was just one long massacre...and it involved immensely exaggerating the scale of Russian intervention.

Orwell, "Looking Back on the Spanish War," pp. 197-8 of A Collection of Essays

This book is a manual for the training of guerrillas in psychological operations, and its application to the concrete case of the Christian and democratic crusade being waged in Nicaragua by the Freedom Commandos.

CIA, last paragraph of Preface

Orwellian Hell

> In any place in which tactical guerrilla operations are carried out in populous areas, the squad should undertake psychological actions parallel to these, and should proceed, accompany and consolidate the common objective and explain to all the people about our struggle, explaining that our presence is to give peace, liberty and democracy to all Nicaraguans without exception, and explaining that our struggle is not against the nationals but rather against Russian imperialism.
>
> CIA, last paragraph of 5.5

The parallels here with Nazi Germany and the Fascists is eerie. The focus on Russian imperialism also rings of the Nazi and Fascist positions in the Spanish Civil War. Ironically, in both instances, the Russians played insignificant roles.

War is Peace

To fully understand war, one must live through a war and experience it personally. Those who find their lives destroyed by war understand it. Those who hear about it from a relative who experienced it can only sympathize, vaguely and abstractly trying to imagine it. Few Americans can truly claim even the latter of these two. Everything most Americans know about war they got from books and the media, and it looks so glorious from a distance. Orwell observed that the authors who dwell most on the horrors of war seldom experienced it for themselves. Why? Those who really experienced war do not want to remember, and those who didn't want to see the glory in it.

Benjamin Franklin once suggested that were chiefs of state to balance the tax revenues over twenty years and the costs of levying war, that they would find it more economical to purchase the property instead. His philosophy could certainly be applied to many war situations, but not to the war for hearts, minds, and markets that has waged since 1945. There is little interest today in taking the property of other nations, but rather in controlling their markets and exhibiting power. Franklin foresaw this later in his brief essay, saying, "But to make and accept such an offer, these potentates should be both of them reasonable creatures, and free from the ambition of glory, which perhaps is too much to be supposed."

The principle "War is Peace" is easily observed. When the US is at relative peace with the rest of the world (relative by perception only, not reality), then it is divided and anarchistic domestically. The moment the public perceives a "threat", the entire population focuses on the threat and attains solidarity. As a consequence, when the US is obviously unstable on the international front, it is stable on the domestic front. This was much less a reality before the Great Depression, when most Americans were not conscious of the Federal government. On the other hand, since WWII, as Orwell observed, this struggle, or gridlock, is the American reality, fitting neatly in with the concept of "Fear is Power". To illustrate, Orwell's hell divides the world into three super states: Oceania, East Asia, and Eurasia. In his hell, these states are in perpetual war, occasionally changing alliances so that at one time Oceania and East Asia are fighting Eurasia, and at another Oceania and Eurasia are fighting against East Asia. This struggle, and other struggles in the story, maintains the peace and solidarity of Oceanians in spite of the oppression. The source of the struggle comes from the ranks of the common person.

Nobody truly wins a war. Everyone loses. Therefore the objective of a just war, meaning one that cannot otherwise be avoided (see my discussions in At War With the White House), is to minimize losses. To win at minimizing losses, one must identify what the objectives of the enemy are. If eliminating the objectives peacefully is not possible, then determine what the weapons are. If eliminating the weapons peacefully is not possible, then determine the targets. Eliminating the targets may be the only solution. Let us look at an example briefly.

In 1938, Gandhi recommended the Jews of Europe commit collective suicide (Orwell, 1946, p. 178). While this sounds absurd on one hand, on the other the people in question were pretty much all secretly tortured to death within the next several years anyway. Had they followed his advice, their suffering would have ended immediately, and world attention would have been drawn to the problem. Of course that would have fulfilled Hitler's sick dream. Personally, I cannot see giving anyone such advice unless I know for certain that it would be the best alternative. On the other hand, Gandhi viewed them as soldiers for their collective cause. In his mind, he did a calculation and determined that the cost of life and suffering would be less than going through with a war, and the radical consequences would have been world attention to the collective protest. This is much like selling property instead of warring over it.

Eliminating the targets does not necessitate destroying the targets. Destroying is violent, whether it is applied to the objectives, weapons, or targets. If you destroy something of your opponent's, then you will only aggravate them further. If you actually destroy your resources, you destroy your people. If you destroy your people, you truly have nothing. For example, the notion of Iraq using a nuclear weapon on Israel is absurd. A nuclear warhead dropped on Jerusalem would turn a large portion of Israel into an extension of the Mediterranean. It would also take out a significant portion of Jordan, and the fallout would spread across Jordan and Iraq. Likewise, poison gasses and biological weapons used on Israel would quickly spread in the same directions. The only use for such weapons, frankly, is for defense against the US and Britain. Otherwise, were Britain and the US not in the neighborhood behaving as international thugs, Iraq would be a local thug. If that local thug posed a real threat, its neighbors would unhesitatingly agree to US and British intervention without having to be paid off in bribes. As the first war with Iraq proved, when the neighbors are upset enough, they are even willing to pay the US and Britain to help. Prime Minister Benjamin Natanyahu states that Israel won't be the first country to introduce nuclear weapons to the Middle East. They would be wise to never acquire nuclear weapons. To do so would be the beginning of their end. Israel must learn to wage peace better than Gandhi did.

To eliminate a thing peacefully, you must remove the desire. In personal life, as I have learned painfully, this means making a sacrifice, sometimes a greater sacrifice than you would ever wish to make. Does this mean there is never a call for violence? In traditional martial arts, the practitioner is forbidden from using their art outside the dojo, punishable by expulsion from the dojos. It is precisely because you have the skill that you should be the bigger person and find a more peaceful solution. Given the state of humanity at present, I regret to say violence is sometimes inescapable. My discussion of using force in At War With the White House need not be reiterated here. One must bear in mind, however, that the ethical measures described here must be applied at every stage of a conflict to assure minimizing losses to both sides and assuring positive outcomes.

Orwell explicitly observed, in 1984, that the struggle of humanity is inevitable. He notes in both 1984 (explicitly) and Animal Farm (implicitly) that the higher class struggles to retain their power, the middle class struggles to get it, and the lower class is so focused on surviving, that they can think of little else. Naturally, the middle class promises the lower class improved living standards to get support to oust the higher class. When this occurs, the classes return to their old ways with simply different faces and names in the upper two. He also notes that the longest-lived governments are institutionally driven, rather than inherited. In 1984, for example, he mentions four key institutions that are independently driven of each other. These are the ministries of Truth (that rewrites history), Peace (the military), Love (espionage), and Plenty (resource management, meaning deprivation). Each of these is necessarily contradictory with themselves and each other, just as the three super states are in perpetual war. To go along with these, science is abolished, except to create weapons to destroy and waste resources, and creativity is focused on anything that will waste away thought through mindless entertainment (not unlike Huxley's <u>Brave New World</u>). The contradictions and empty entertainment encourage ignorance, which is the basis of the strength. Consider how these concepts apply to the present world, and a shudder should come up your spine. This leads to the next topic.

Ignorance is Strength

The main character of 1984, Winston, works in the "Ministry of Truth" which is really a ministry of misinformation. Truth, in popular opinion, is fact. On the contrary, truth is based on belief and has nothing to do with fact. That is why Winston's job was to rewrite history favorably for Big Brother, and to develop appropriate propaganda around that history. He can make heroes out of villains, he can burn down non-existent villages, and dictate the number of casualties. For all he knows, the information he is tweaking was tweaked before. In fact, he is certain much of it is, because some he remembers tweaking before himself. His job is to retain the level of ignorance, and thereby retain the strength of popular support for Big Brother. By doing this, people could simply chalk up memories as misled, and form a new belief, a new truth.

After September 11 (2001), the DOD and Justice Department wanted to create an office for managing the press. This had all the appearances of a Ministry of Truth. This created such an uproar, that eventually it was announced that the department would not be created. Now ask yourself this: if you wanted to create a ministry of truth, would you want the population to know? If the population found out, wouldn't claiming that you are not going to create it after all be great camouflage to actually doing so? I don't want to turn you into a paranoiac, but the logic is scary. What is scarier is that the department actually exists, and has since 1948. The Office of Policy Coordination was created in 1948. It is a covert wing of the CIA responsible for "propaganda, economic warfare, preventive direct action, including sabotage, anti-sabotage, demolition and evacuation procedures; subversion against hostile states, including assistance to underground resistance groups, and support of indigenous anti-communist elements in threatened countries of the free world." Associated with this, the CIA started Operation Mockingbird to create "assets" out of news agencies and journalists. Spin doctors are so well known of, that political science textbooks tell you all about them, and there are plenty of examples in the movies (a prime example is Wag the Dog).

While we are easily misinformed, we are fortunate that the world has not gone to the extremity of Orwell's "Ministry of Truth". The CIA used to chase after leaks. Now, the Internet and the constant flood of leaks into the press make this impossible. Now the CIA has to count on too much information, and spinning what appears on the cover of newspapers and magazines. If you want to know what is really going on, don't read the headlines. Start reading no earlier than A8 in the newspaper. If this were your habit, in 1943 you would have read all about the Holocaust in Germany. In more recent history, you would know British Commandos fired the first shots of the war in Afghanistan. If Americans had shot first, it would be on the front pages of the papers.

I know it is the fashion to say that most of recorded history is lies anyway. I am willing to believe that history is for the most part inaccurate and biased, but what is peculiar to our own age is the abandonment of the idea that history *could* be truthfully written. In the past people deliberately lied, or they unconsciously coloured what they wrote, or they struggled after the truth, well knowing that they must make many mistakes; but in each case they believed that "the facts" existed and were more or less discoverable.... A British and a German historian would disagree deeply on many things, even on fundamentals [of the World War I], but there would still be that body of, as it were, neutral fact on which neither would seriously challenge the other. It is just this common basis of agreement, with its implication that human beings are all one

145

species of animal, that totalitarianism destroys. Nazi theory indeed specifically denies that such a thing as "truth" exists. There is, for instance, no such thing as "Science." There is only "German Science," "Jewish Science," etc. The implied objective of this line of thought is a nightmare world in which the Leader, or some ruling clique, controls not only the future but *the past*. If the Leader says of such and such an event, "It never happened"—well, it never happened. If he says that two and two are five—well, two and two are five. This prospect frightens me more than bombs—and after our experiences [with the Blitz of London] of the last few years that is not a frivolous statement.

George Orwell (Looking Back on the Spanish War, 1943)

in A Collection of Essays, p. 199; author's emphases

Orwell brings up two crucial points in this brief passage. First, people choose ignorance by displacing reality with entertainment. Orwell specifies "football" (soccer in England) just to make his point. Let me be a little more specific. First, entertainment in general is a form of escape from reality, and much that we have in modern society. We slaves leave work and listen to the radio with the bad news of the car accidents, and music to escape the reality of traffic. We get home and submerse ourselves in more violence and fantasy. Football, soccer, boxing, hockey, and wrestling are all violent sports. News focuses on the bloodiest and goriest details, numbing us to violence. So-called reality shows allow people to imagine themselves competing in some remote region of the world to win large sums of money and become celebrities. Talk shows tell us that other families are even more dysfunctional than our own, and it is okay. After being reprogrammed by the media, we summarily turn to bed so we can begin the process over. Meanwhile, our children are going through basically the same routine, only because the parents are such slaves, the children are forced to face these false realities alone and with little explanation, and the schools do not help.

We are programmed to do as we are told and believe what we are told to believe. Teachers are under extreme scrutiny. They dare not teach the facts, not even if the parents demand it. They can only teach the popular truth the administration wants them to teach (which is to a lesser degree also true in colleges). If it were popular to say $2 + 2 = 5$, then math teachers would have to rewrite their textbooks and teach accordingly. The only hope for a real education is for the student to experience harsh reality first, and then enter a college where faculty members are relatively free from administrative control and actually care about students more than their own research.

While I am reluctant to paint such a bleak picture of the modern world, like Aristotle, I am dismayed by the quality of students, namely the apathy, and my observations of the rest of the world situation give me no more positive position. On the other hand, by documenting the qualities of our living hell, it is my hope that we, as citizens, will gain the knowledge we need to pull our heads out of the sand and see what is really happening. When that occurs, then we stand a chance of escaping this hell, and building a safe world in which our children may live prosperously.

Freedom is Slavery

We are free to go about our lives, make money, spend, and work ourselves into debt. The spending and debt make us slaves to work. Frankly, slaves were often treated better than the employees of today. Employers feel they can do anything they want with labor; because there is always someone else they can hire to replace you. Slaves, on the other hand, are property. If you abuse slaves, then you damage their value, and it costs money to replace them. We live in the illusion of freedom. Even as a master, you are a slave, because being the master requires enormous maintenance, so the master becomes a slave to the system and the struggle to retain power. In 1984, Orwell explicitly observes this throughout the story. The proles are free to do what they like with relatively little supervision. Because they are ignorant, their opinions simply don't matter. Those who aren't ignorant are identified and eventually neutralized, to use a modern term. On the other hand, Party members are scrutinized every moment by the Secret Police. They must be intelligent yet live in the contradictions of the system. They must agree with the party position unhesitatingly, to the point that the agreement comes before it is known that such an agreement should exist. In Orwell's hell, those in power and those in the disputed territories are really the ones who suffer. The working class proles are the fortunate ones, because at least they can live their ignorant lives and not even be conscious of the conflict around them.

In Orwell's hell, Oceania is nowhere near free. Life of a Party member is so regulated, that the wake up call is immediately followed by an exercise regime, love is forbidden except among the lowest of society, and everyone is watched for thought crime by secret police through the visi-screens. While the US proclaims to have certain of these rights, it holds to them only when the US is not otherwise offended. Heaven forbid the truth should ever reach the population. Ellsberg knows this experience too well, and is a fortunate survivor to tell his story. We tend to look too closely at 1984, and not realize how much really does apply to us. Let us take a moment and consider that idea.

We are also free to take the path of crime, until we are caught. In the land of the "free" we have more of our citizens incarcerated than any other society throughout history. So much for our freedom, or in the words of Kurt Vonnegut, "So it goes." In a capitalist society we live in an illusion of freedom. In reality, we are slaves to taxes, consumerism, and the ignorance of the masses. Go to any university law library (which typically takes up a building) and just look at the countless law books. Lao Tse once said that more laws are a sure sign of a lack of morality. They are also a symbol of freedoms lost. They are not freedoms lost for the wealthy, or those who construct them, but they are a loss to everyone else. If you have the fortune of having referendum on your ballot, think very closely before you approve the passage of any law. NOWHERE IS IT WRITTEN that you must vote on everything on the ballot. My rules are simple. Amendments to the Constitution are automatically "no", unless I can see the overarching impact is meaningful and can last forever. Most Amendments should frankly be statutes, as they lack the durability of time and potentially impact unrelated matters. I look skeptically on any potential statute, and if I know nothing about it, I do not vote on it. Why should I? Even though I go out of my way to study these things, I cannot know everything. Nor can you. So long as it has no impact on me, I will simply leave it blank for those who are impacted. Beware what freedoms you vote yourself out of.

Conclusion

Our argument holds that the true axis of evil is not third world nations with their weapons of mass destruction or terrorists. The true axis of evil are the powers that instigate third world nations to resort to these means out of desperation to either escape oppression or defend against it. We of the first world need to look in our own back yards for the true axis of evil, and eradicate our own evil ways. We have the capacity to do this, as our next chapter will show, and thereby overcome this Orwellian hell we have constructed for ourselves.

Israel is not far behind the US, but mostly on a local level. Britain is frankly tagging along for the ride. The United States is living the world of George Orwell's 1984—manipulate the masses with constant fear of external threats, leading them into being the unwitting perpetrators of aggression. Orwell's genius is observing this condition of humanity as exploited by a government desperate for power. In Orwell's world, Oceania is a horrifying place to live, but the government keeps the people in control with the fear of outside enemies who are supposedly worse. This works for any government, and in the US works marvelously with an over-anxious media vying for the dollars acquired by selling their news and keeping the population in fear so they want to buy more. The US, in essence, behaves like a mafia don, having others get their hands dirty, then fingering, neglecting, or outright turning against them later to take the heat off the real source. This argument makes evident that the biggest enemy we have against terrorism is ourselves. If we wish to overcome this enemy, then we must learn the lessons Orwell teaches, and overcome the obstacles of our form of government. The nature of the US government is in many ways optimum. What most greatly reduces its capacity for doing the right thing is the culture and selective ignorance we choose. So long as we allow our fears to control us, then ignorance will dominate, and power will be abused.

Steps Toward A Solution

Introduction

It is my view, and a point of contention I have with other writers on this topic, that if one is to offer a criticism, one should also offer solutions. Failure to offer reasonable and peaceful solutions will only inspire more radical violence, with the same ultimate outcomes as Orwell observes. In this chapter we will examine how we live in a world filled with illusions and opportunities. The greatest obstacle of solving the problem of terrorism is overcoming the political illusions of modern society. This obstacle, as any obstacle, is also our greatest opportunity. The method of Aikido fits our objectives here. The method is simple. First, we observe where the aggression is. Second, we find a constructive use for that energy and direct it accordingly. In other words, we find a non-violent solution to violence.

Political Illusions

Failure to recognize the controlling government as perceived by populations is a critical error in today's world politics. As a rule, on the international front, governments are recognized for reasons having nothing to do with the people governed. As such, you have cells of people who do not recognize the internationally recognized government of their region. This creates obvious friction, as the internationally recognized government is trapped in a power struggle with the government preferred and/or recognized by the people. Typically we look on this as revolutionary, while we Americans like to forget that at one time we fostered the same feelings toward England, and that we projected those feelings in the Monroe Doctrine against other European powers and their colonial efforts in the Americas.

Our concern is to dissect the true nature of existing, recognized political systems. Here we will dive into communism, capitalism, and dictatorships. You will note that only one of these, dictatorship, when treated, is not labeled pseudo, indicating that it is held genuinely as would be expected.

Dictatorship

The dictatorship is perhaps the simplest form of government to understand. Fundamentally the philosophical perspectives of dictators range from absolutely self-serving to absolutely benevolent. Benevolent dictators are enormously rare, but can also be extremely ruthless. Typically the weight is thrown more toward self-serving than benevolent. Since the self-serving dictatorship is the one where trouble will occur, particularly crimes against humanity, we will focus on it.

The self-serving dictator cares about only one thing: his or her own personal wealth and power. Frankly, I cannot recall a situation where a self-serving dictator was a woman, so we will continue using only the "he" pronoun. A person living in this type of dictatorship has nearly unlimited freedom. The only time that freedom is restricted is when it violates the personal desires of the dictator. How is it, then, that this is the most likely place for human rights violations? The answer is in the nature of the beast. The self-serving dictator will do anything to absorb the resources of his population.

Every dictator is clearly aware of a simple fact: they own absolutely everything, including the people. An intelligent dictator understands the social contract and is careful with the extent to which they abuse their ownership. An intelligent dictator also knows that the better they treat their people, the more wealthy everyone is. Unfortunately, passing an IQ test and training in political science are not prerequisites to becoming a dictator. Consequently, dictators do not typically have the tools they need to be effective in fulfilling their desires.

Dictators today fall into one of three categories: heritage, military, and revolutionary. The dictator who acquired the position through lineage (heritage) will typically also have a great deal of preparation for the job.

They are people, however, and just because they are born there and receive the training does not make them any more competent than the next dictator. On the other hand, they may have paid attention to the wrong lessons, and thereby learned the fine art of spinning (media manipulation). The revolutionary dictator is most likely an idealist, and likely to follow a path toward totalitarianism. The revolutionary is also likely to become similar to a military dictator, leaning against foreign powers for support, training, and finances. In these instances, the dictator becomes a puppet of the foreign power. Some foolish dictators have made the mistake of challenging their roles as puppets and found their support immediately withdrawn, resulting in almost assured change in regime.

The military dictator is very often a puppet as described above. Typically this person came to power because of a coup. Most coups are inspired, funded, armed, trained, and otherwise supported by foreign powers. This person is no more of a state head than any other military person. Military people are taught to obey orders, then later to supervise a disciplined community (soldiers). This does not work well when applied to a general population. If this person is a hero of the people, then there is sure to be trouble with the foreign powers that supported the coup. Any hero of the people of his own country is definitely more interested in his domestic matters than the economy of a foreign nation.

Aristocratic Pseudo-Communism

By aristocratic pseudo-communism, I am referring to the real nature of the so-called communist countries of the 20th and 21st centuries. The reason these are pseudo-communist countries is that they really aren't communist. They do, however, borrow some ideals from the theory of communism. Because these are governments based on an idea, which at least in the beginning is inflicted on the people, these governments tend to a degree of totalitarianism. Totalitarianism is similar to a dictatorship taken to an extreme. Where a dictator is likely to be selfish, the totalitarian is extremely selfless. The totalitarian is concerned about creating a greater good bigger than himself, so he is an idealist. As an idealist, he wants to see his idea implemented. Of course that means that voices of descent must be silenced. Totalitarian governments are characterized by this idea of total control, meaning controlling everything including thought. Totalitarian governments have typically been experiments in forms of communism. As such, let us examine the qualities of true communism:

- All resources are equally distributed. In other words, the floor sweeper makes as much as the rocket scientist, the doctor, the actor or singer, or the professional sportsman.
- Everyone is taken care of, and the able-bodied all have work.
- The nation owns all enterprises, and is owned by the people. This is a critical issue that conflicts with the next.
- Everyone has equal opportunity. This is misleading; nationalization also means you have the same boss no matter where you go. Once you pick the career, that is it.
- Everyone has equal say in the government (this is not applied as seen below), which of course means the people have to agree with the ideology of communism, which also necessitates...
- Everyone is educated and literate, or at least given the greatest opportunity to be so. We note that literacy in "communist" countries exceeds other nations, including the US and Britain.

These fundamental ideals look remarkably like the values of democracy. In fact, they are the values of democracy taken to their ultimate extreme. These values do not work with humans. Not only is there an issue with the availability of resources to make this possible, but human motivations simply don't agree. H.G. Wells wrote extensively against utopias, and communism of course is a utopian idea. In each instance he found his utopias to be living hells, with only one exception: Men Like Gods. It is, as Cicero states, the exception that proves the rule. The book itself is not enormously compelling to read, however, Wells does exhibit his enormous intelligence and insight. He realized the only way to get a utopia to work without losing humanity is if you change a critical quality of humanity. The society in which Wells shows perfect communism working is motivated by self-actualization needs, meaning they are motivated by the love of knowledge and the love of what they do. Food is not an issue in his society, nor do people feel unsafe or insecure in their environments. People simply get along because they all have the same type of motivation, and thereby are respectful. The same also causes that there are no titles of esteem. Basically he describes a society of an inverted hierarchy of Abraham Maslow's needs. This is not something that can be achieved by force. It is attainable only through education that spans generations. From what I see throughout history, only a massive catastrophe that affects all the people in the world could possibly motivate such an end. Such an end would actually be a significant evolutionary step for our species.

We have established that true communism has never been attained, and likely never will, at least not with humans in their present state. As such, when communism has been attempted, it has required much modification. First, those who try to implement it don't like applying the rules to themselves. This is only normal, because people think, "rules are there to protect me from others" rather than, "rules are there to protect others from me." Next, those who try to implement realize there are various degrees of support, and they need to reward those degrees appropriately; therefore, they get some relief from the rules also, depending on their support. In the end, we observe that every "communist" system is really socialism applied to the working caste, with various levels of aristocracy in a ruling caste. So much for communism.

Capitalist Pseudo-Democracy

Like communism, the idea of democracy is equally brilliant, equally flawed, and likewise not really accomplished. Democratic institutions are an illusion of civilian government. We have a tendency to call them "representative democracies", which is equally misleading. Occasionally a common person is actually able to penetrate the caste of the ruling class, but that is the unusual exception. Like dictators who acquire their power from revolution or coup, elected "leaders" tend to require backing from the real leadership, which is mostly industry and the wealthy.

About this illusion...The illusion works so well because the people perceive their role in government. Take, as an example, the American presidency. In my lifetime, I do not recall a single election in which I felt satisfied with my choice of candidates. I hear similar complaints from people all the time. In spite of this, we Americans stand by our leadership because, after all, even if we didn't vote for this guy, we voted. Therefore all is well. Besides, if we really hate him, we can vote him out soon. As history shows, tragedy and war equal power if they are managed even half-heartedly. Throw one or both on the worst possible candidate and guess what...they're up for reelection. Everything else is brushed under the rug.

So democracy is also a failure. What about capitalism? Capitalism is also a brilliant idea with a significant character flaw. Ironically it has the same character flaw as communism: motivation. Lets speak frankly, as if I haven't already. Most people will define the American dream as "getting the most (wealth, power, whatever) from the least (effort, expense, etc.)." This single statement is a religious experience to the capitalist of every rank. The guy at the bottom wants to be arbitrarily put on top. The guy on top wants to remain or is greedy and wants more. This is a society based on greed. America is a lawless (for those who can afford the right attorneys) vat of cannibalistic snakes. Don't let the countless documented laws fool you. They are written by the snakes to either protect or arm themselves in the struggle. Being a person who tends to call things as I see them, it is very likely you are a snake. Don't feel bad. I am one too. So what can we do? It is every American's duty to educate themselves and participate in the election system. Given the obstacles I will add the famous words of Thoreau: Cast your whole vote.

World Government

As I write, the world is roughly divided into three existing super powers (US, Russia, China), one emerging super power (the European Union), allies of these super powers, and the exploited third world. As a rule, the common American lives under the misconception that the US is the top dog. They forget that China, with ¼ of the world's population, handily whipped us along with 19 other countries before they had established themselves and before their military was modernized. They also forget that Russia still has the power of the former USSR, only without the buffer zones. The EU, with its 700 million people that is quickly growing, is easily on par with the US in technology, and if its military were unified (which is soon likely) then the US (with only 250 million people) would be running up with China for 3rd place (a judgment that would be based solely on technology, not manpower). Only a fool would underestimate the potentials of the super powers. As Orwell foresaw, these super powers are next to impervious to each other, even if two got together to gang up on a third.

The nations are all unfairly represented in the United Nations. The Marshall Islands, for example, has the same vote in the general assembly as China. The consensus around the world is that the US really holds all the cards in the UN, and this is fundamentally true. On one hand the US emphasizes the need to abide by international law, and then flagrantly violates the same. The UN is virtually hog-tied and unable to do anything about it. On the other hand, were the nations of the world wise, they could take control of the UN and empower it sensibly.

To empower the UN sensibly, one would first have to eliminate the charter and set up something more equitable, such as Madison's model that became the US constitution. By using such a model, individual nations would not be directly represented. Instead, populations would be represented. Nations, like the states in early American history, want desperately to retain their sovereignty. The opportunity cost is safety. The only way a real UN could function would be to allow a degree of independence to each nation just as a degree of independence is given to each state. The difference would be obvious: no more arms buildup, no more war.

History shows that the longest-lived societies are based on an ideal of balanced bureaucracies. On the smallest scale, pure democracy is possible; on a large scale only representative democracy is practical. On a large scale, bureaucratic branches of equal power balance each other out. When the people feel they are fairly represented, they tend to be satisfied. When a people's security is in question, particularly if they are desperate, they lose confidence in their leadership, and the risk of violence erupts. Here, democracy offers competition for power, which gives the people the opportunity to select someone they have more confidence in. What is missing is real equal opportunity.

As a student, I realized that getting a degree was a right of passage for which one paid a given amount, regurgitated what one was told, and basically served a sentence. Fortunately, I was driven to learn at an early age, and learned in spite of my education; but I am an extreme exception to the general rules. As a teacher, I have grappled with this issue, because I naturally expect education to occur. How silly of me to foster such a notion when the students are bent on fulfilling their right of passage. Any teacher will tell you that a student who actually embraces learning is the exception to the rule. The rule is that people are comfortable in their ignorance, and will defend their ignorance. Another rule in education that people neglect is the true nature of education. Education is not passive. A teacher cannot open the student's head and pour the information in, though we wish we could. Learning occurs only when the student is motivated to put in the effort, and is otherwise accidental.

Why must I grapple with such issues? The reason is simple, and dependent on the audience in question. Those from the lowest levels of society know that in spite of the right of passage, they will achieve little more than mediocrity. Those in the middle, who are typically older students, are the most motivated and prove to be the most common exception, and only because they have a love for knowledge, not for other gains. Those from the highest levels of society know they need not accomplish anything, because it will be given to them anyway. There is no true motivation to getting a good education, because equal opportunity is an illusion.

When China adopted Confucianism as the state orthodoxy, a system of tests was implemented. Anyone from any level of society could learn and take the examinations that would accelerate them into the ranks of the government. What I have observed of American examinations for government jobs is nothing short of a joke. Basically, if you can read and paid any attention through the eighth grade, you can pass the examination. Often a requirement for a degree is attached, but nowhere in the degree was there a real expectation that learning actually occurred. Illiteracy among college students is truly shocking. Ironically, to run for office there is few restrictions. The most common restriction is the ability to raise the money to do the campaign. This has absolutely nothing to do with aptitude or psychological readiness. As such, it takes nothing for a well-connected (meaning born into the right family) and psychotic person to take office. Not only does there need to be examinations for competence, there needs to be psychological profiling done so the people are able to choose a candidate based on ability rather than on who can rally the most wealth. If this were the case, and education would be accessible equally and freely (rather than spending trillions on weapons to encourage war against us), then students would really care about their learning, because they would have real opportunities instead of illusions.

Another issue Orwell mentioned in 1984 was the locus of control. In 1984, Oceania has a decentralized government, meaning no central capital. Oceania's government is driven universally by the same ideology and concepts, but the leadership is nearly invisible and drawn from the local community. Assuming my above recommendation is followed, then the caste system of Oceania would not exist, and the idea of waging perpetual peace could prevail (which Orwell notes would be an easy replacement for perpetual war). When the government is invisible to the common person, except when the common person needs the government to help, then the government is functioning properly. Unfortunately, this is often taken as an opportunity for the press to muckrake the personal lives of otherwise effective leaders and expose their human mistakes that have nothing to do with their jobs and efficiency (see the War is Peace argument).

This brings us to the next observation: media and artistic ethics. In an effort to make money, media and entertainment focus on the sensational without regard to the consequences on society. This is a search for immediate gratification. If the entire entertainment industry decided to act ethically, they would find sales falter slightly for a while, but then they would bounce back because people want to be entertained. In my recent book, The Legend of PŭMa Tse, I showed that a compelling ethical story could be told without resorting to violence. In another recent book, Daniel 13: The Therapist, I used violence constructively to show the absurdity of the human condition, but it is all a struggle within the mind of an individual. These are stories with ethical themes, not stories written to be current box office smashes. The current box office smash has no real story. It is filled with violence, sensationalism, flat characters, and lacks any compelling theme to attract mature audiences. How can an audience mature if the only thing they have for entertainment is so shallow? If the entertainment industry wants to survive and prosper for another century, they need to ask themselves these questions and strive toward building a society receptive to entertainment, rather than destroyed by its fears and progressive violence it learned from the entertainment.

Conclusion

We live under the illusions of perfect government. The mentality of "us and them," where we are good and they are necessarily evil, is promulgated by the entertainment industry. We are our worst enemies, and in the modern world, we are a species capable of overcoming this mentality. We are in an age of great opportunities. We need only exploit these opportunities, demand them as a species and accept our brethren as equal under the skin. Anything less promotes the continuation of the atrocities we are accountable for. We can be civilized and make the right choice, or live in the misery we create. Should we choose the misery, let's at least be honest enough to recognize our own contribution to it. Should we choose the civilized, peaceful alternative, then we should first acknowledge that no-one is above the law, and when we are called to be fearful and promote atrocities, we refuse to participate in that fear and thereby remove the power from those who use it to exploit us. The issues surrounding world government and waging peace are clearly too broad and involved for this study, so I will reserve them for later consumption.

Post Script

While the rest of this chapter is certainly worthy of debate, none of it adequately solves the real problems. The real problems are as subtle as our definitions for winning and success, detachment from actual resources and food sources, over-dependence on technology and degrading attention (demand for immediate closure). The real problems are so systemic that nothing in this book can really solve them. Another book is currently in the works (A Sustainable World Order) that will outline the general solution as an institution of objective focus called Akademé. Unfortunately, the right path will not be chosen without great sacrifices and sufferings. Along the path from absolutely wrong thinking to workably correct thinking guided by Akademé, elements in this and other chapters will certainly be relevant. The trick with the solution is to keep social

Steps Toward A Solution

evolution on track despite its mistakes, while limiting the impact of those mistakes without judgment.

Bibliography

Bard, M.G. (2001). Myths and Facts: A Guide to Arab-Israeli Conflict. Chevy Chase, MD: Arab-Israeli Cooperative Alliance.

Benson, S. (August 4, 2002). "The Bomb Made Us War Criminals." The Arizona Republic. Phoenix, AZ.

Blum, W. (1995). Killing Hope: US Military and CIA Interventions since World War II. Monroe, ME: Common Courage Press.

Boas, P. (August 4, 2002). "We Put a Final End to a Horrible War." The Arizona Republic. Phoenix, AZ: Republic and Gazette.

Chomsky, N. (2001). 9/11. New York, NY: Seven Stories Press.

Chomsky, N. (1996). World Orders Old and New. New York, NY: Columbia University Press.

Chomsky, N. (1988). Manufacturing Consent: The Political Economy of the Mass Media. New York, NY: Pantheon Books.

Davidson, P.B. (1988). Vietnam at War: the history 1946-1975. New York: Oxford University Press.

Ellsberg, D. (2002). Secrets: A Memoir of Vietnam and the Pentagon Papers. New York, NY: Viking.

Grunn, B. (1991). The Timetables of History. 3 ed. New York, NY: Simon & Schuster/Touchstone.

Kangas, S. A Timeline of CIA Atrocities. Retrieved on February 13, 2003 from http://www.korpios.org/resurgent/CIATimeline.html.

McCarthy, C. (December 13, 1987). "The Consequences of Covert Tactics" Washington Post.

McGehee, R. (October 9, 1999). CIA Support of Death Squads. Retrieved on February 13, 2003 from http://serendipity.magnet.ch/cia/death_squads.htm

Orwell, G. (1949). 1984. http://orwell.ru/library/novels/1984/e/e1984_1a.htm.

Orwell, G. (1981). A Collection of Essays. San Diego, CA: Harvest Books.

Bibliography

Orwell, G. <u>Fifty Orwell Essays</u>. Australia: Project Guttenberg.
  http://www.gutenberg.net.au/ebooks03/0300011.txt.

Orwell, G. (1945). <u>Animal Farm: A Fairy Story</u>.
  http://orwell.ru/library/novels/Animal_Farm/e/i_ii.htm.

School of the America's Watch. http://www.soaw.org/

Vankin, Jonathan and John Whalen. (1997). <u>The 60 Greatest Conspiracies
  of All Time</u>. Secaucus, N.J.: Citadel Press.

Waller, D. (February 3, 2003). "The CIA's Secret Army" (Cover Story).
  <u>Time Magazine</u>. http://www.time.com/time/covers/1101030203/.

Wells, H.G. <u>Men Like Gods</u>. Australia: Project Guttenberg.
  http://www.gutenberg.net.au/0200221.txt.

Useful Sources

Any search of the Internet for topics mentioned here will typically land a
goldmine of information. It is not a matter of insufficient data, merely
general ignorance of the colossal amount out there. Always be careful with
the sources you examine, though even the shady ones need to have some
element of truth to them. Always double check, and seek the most
reputable sources. Once you start getting an idea of how the patterns
function in the world, then you can set your browser to
http://www.cnn.com/WORLD/ and see what is going on in each region. You
will be shocked at what is being brushed under the carpet to be replaced
by the six-car pile-up on the freeway this afternoon and the weather man's
basket weaving course. Whatever you do, don't stop at the headlines. I
advise my students to start at A8 of the major newspapers and begin
reading there. Don't even bother with the headlines. The following are also
useful:

<u>Derechos Humanas en America Latina</u>. http://www.derechos.org/nizkor/la/.
  In Spanish, English is different.

<u>New York Times</u>. http://query.nytimes.com/search/advanced

<u>Time Magazine</u>. http://www.time.com/time/magazine/archives/advanced

Washington Post. http://www.washingtonpost.com/wp-adv/archives/front.htm

Washington Times. http://www.washtimes.com/archives.htm

Z Magazine. http://zena.secureforum.com/znet/zmag/zmag.cfm reached through http://zmag.org

Appendix A

Per Year Involvement

This table, and the next, list most foreign entanglements the US has been involved in between 1890 and 2002. The table shows not only the quantity but the quality of military involvement. You will note that neither world war is included, and Hawaii was an independent nation. Notes: ‡ Bloodless, * Failed.

Year	Country	Category
1890	Argentina	Military Intervention
1891	Chile	Military Intervention
1891	Haiti	Military Intervention
1893	Hawaii	Military Intervention
1894	Nicaragua	Military Intervention
1894-95	China	Military Intervention
1894-96	Korea	Military Intervention
1895	Panama	Military Intervention
1896	Nicaragua	Military Intervention
1898	Nicaragua	Military Intervention
1898-	Puerto Rico	Military Intervention and occupied
1898-	Guam	Military Intervention and occupied
1898-1900	China	Military Intervention
1898-1902	Cuba	Military Intervention
1898-1939	Philippines	Occupied
1899	Nicaragua	Military Intervention
1899-	Samoa	Occupied
1901-14	Panama	Military Intervention
1903	Honduras	Military Intervention
1903-04	Dominican Republic	Military Intervention
1904-05	Korea	Military Intervention
1906-09	Cuba	Military Intervention
1907	Honduras	Military Intervention
1907	Nicaragua	Military Intervention
1908	Panama	Military Intervention

Appendix A

1910	Nicaragua	Military Intervention
1911	Honduras	Military Intervention
1911-41	China	Military Intervention
1912	Cuba	Military Intervention
1912	Honduras	Military Intervention
1912	Panama	Military Intervention
1912-33	Nicaragua	Military Intervention
1913	Mexico	Military Intervention
1914	Dominican Republic	Military Intervention
1914-18	Mexico	Military Intervention
1914-34	Haiti	Military Intervention
1916-24	Dominican Republic	Military Intervention
1917-33	Cuba	Military Intervention
1918-20	Panama	Military Intervention
1918-22	Russia	Military Intervention
1919	Dominican Republic	Invasion
1919	Haiti	Invasion
1919	Honduras	Military Intervention
1919	Yugoslavia	Military Intervention
1920	Guatemala	Military Intervention
1920	Venezuela	Invasion
1922	Turkey	Military Intervention
1922-27	China	Military Intervention
1924-25	Honduras	Military Intervention
1925	Panama	Military Intervention
1927-34	China	Military Intervention
1932	El Salvador	Military Intervention
1945-54	Vietnam	Aided, supported, and eventually paid for French re-colonization
1946	Iran	Military Intervention
1946	Yugoslavia	Attack
1947	Uruguay	Threatened Attack
1947-49	Greece	Military Intervention
1948	Germany	Military Intervention
1948-49	China	Military Intervention
1948-54	Philippines	Military Intervention

1950	Puerto Rico	Military Intervention
1950-	South Korea	Occupied
1950-53	Korea	Military Intervention
1953	Iran	CIA coup
1954	Guatemala	CIA coup
1954	Guatemala	Attack
1954	Vietnam	Threatened Attack (nuclear)
1954-64	Vietnam	Covert action throughout Vietnam, post-French
1956	Egypt	Threatened Attack
1958	Cambodia	Attack
1958	China	Threatened Attack
1958	Indonesia	Revolt, CIA inspired *
1958	Iran	Threatened Attack
1958	Laos	Elections sabotaged
1958	Lebanon	Military Intervention
1958	Myanmar	Government undermined
1958	Panama	Military Intervention
1959	Cuba	Attack
1959	Haiti	Military Intervention
1961	Cuba	Invasion *
1961	Dominican Republic	Assassination
1961	Ecuador	CIA coup ‡
1961	El Salvador	CIA coup ‡
1961	Germany	Military Intervention
1961	Vietnam	Attack in South Vietnam (poison gas)
1961	Zaire	Assassination
1962	Cuba	Invasion *
1962	Laos	Military Intervention
1962	Venezuela	Invasion *
1963	Dominican Republic	CIA coup
1963	Ecuador	CIA coup
1963	Vietnam	CIA coup in South Vietnam
1964	Brazil	CIA coup
1964	Panama	Military Intervention
1964-75	Vietnam	"Vietnam War"

Appendix A

1965	Dominican Republic	Military Intervention
1965	Greece	Regime change, forced
1965	Indonesia	CIA coup
1965	Zaire	CIA coup
1965-66	Dominican Republic	Military Intervention
1966-67	Guatemala	Military Intervention
1967	Greece	CIA coup
1969-75	Cambodia	Military Intervention
1970	Cambodia	Regime change, forced
1970	Oman	Indirect (via Iran) Invasion
1971	Bolivia	CIA coup
1971-73	Laos	Attack
1973	Chile	CIA coup
1975	Australia	Regime change, forced
1975	Cambodia	Military Intervention
1976-92	Angola	Revolt, CIA inspired
1979	El Salvador	CIA coup
1980	Iran	Attack *
1980	Iran	Military Intervention
1981	Libya	Attack
1981	Nicaragua	Revolt, CIA inspired
1981-90	Nicaragua	Revolt, CIA inspired
1981-92	El Salvador	Military Intervention
1982	Lebanon	Invasion
1982-84	Lebanon	Military Intervention
1983	Grenada	Invasion
1983-84	Grenada	Occupied
1983-89	Honduras	Military Intervention
1984	Iran	Attack
1986	Bolivia	Military Intervention
1986	Libya	Attack
1986	Libya	Attack
1987-88	Iran	Attack
1989	Libya	Attack
1989	Panama	Military Intervention
1989	Philippines	Military Intervention

1989-90	Panama	Invasion
1990	Liberia	Military Intervention
1991	Haiti	CIA coup
1991	Iran	Invasion
1992-2002	Iran	Attack
1992-94	Somalia	Military Intervention
1992-94	Yugoslavia	Military Intervention
1993-95	Bosnia	Military Intervention
1994-96	Haiti	Military Intervention
1995	Croatia	Military Intervention
1996	Iran	CIA coup *
1996-97	Zaire	Military Intervention
1997	Albania	Military Intervention
1997	Liberia	Military Intervention
1998	Afghanistan	Attack
1998	Sudan	Attack
1999	Yugoslavia	Attack
2000	Peru	CIA coup *
2000	Yemen	Attack
2001	Eritrea	CIA coup *
2001	Macedonia	Military Intervention
2002	Venezuela	CIA coup *

‡ Bloodless
* Failed

Involvement by Country

Notes: ‡ Bloodless, * Failed.

Country	Year	Category
Afghanistan	1998	Attack
Albania	1997	Military Intervention
Angola	1976-92	Revolt, CIA inspired
Argentina	1890	Military Intervention
Australia	1975	Regime change, forced
Bolivia	1971	CIA coup
	1986	Military Intervention
Bosnia	1993-95	Military Intervention
Brazil	1964	CIA coup

Appendix A

Cambodia	1969-75	Military Intervention
	1958	Attack
	1970	Regime change, forced
	1975	Military Intervention
Chile	1891	Military Intervention
	1973	CIA coup
China	1898-1900	Military Intervention
	1894-95	Military Intervention
	1911-41	Military Intervention
	1927-34	Military Intervention
	1922-27	Military Intervention
	1948-49	Military Intervention
	1958	Threatened Attack
Croatia	1995	Military Intervention
Cuba	1898-1902	Military Intervention
	1917-33	Military Intervention
	1906-09	Military Intervention
	1912	Military Intervention
	1959	Attack
	1961	Invasion *
	1962	Invasion *
Dominican Republic	1916-24	Military Intervention
	1903-04	Military Intervention
	1965-66	Military Intervention
	1914	Military Intervention
	1919	Invasion
	1961	Assassination
	1963	CIA coup
	1965	Military Intervention
Ecuador	1961	CIA coup ‡
	1963	CIA coup
Egypt	1956	Threatened Attack
El Salvador	1981-92	Military Intervention
	1932	Military Intervention
	1961	CIA coup ‡
	1979	CIA coup
Eritrea	2001	CIA coup *
Germany	1948	Military Intervention

	1961	Military Intervention
Greece	1947-49	Military Intervention
	1965	Regime change, forced
	1967	CIA coup
Grenada	1983-84	Occupied
	1983	Invasion
Guam	1898-	Military Intervention and occupied
Guatemala	1966-67	Military Intervention
	1920	Military Intervention
	1954	CIA coup
	1954	Attack
Haiti	1914-34	Military Intervention
	1891	Military Intervention
	1994-96	Military Intervention
	1919	Invasion
	1959	Military Intervention
	1991	CIA coup
Hawaii	1893 (-?)	Military Intervention
Honduras	1983-89	Military Intervention
	1924-25	Military Intervention
	1903	Military Intervention
	1907	Military Intervention
	1911	Military Intervention
	1912	Military Intervention
	1919	Military Intervention
Indonesia	1958	Revolt, CIA inspired *
	1965	CIA coup
Iran	1987-88	Attack
	1946	Military Intervention
	1953	CIA coup
	1980	Attack *
	1980	Military Intervention
	1984	Attack
	1992-2002	Attack
	1958	Threatened Attack
	1991	Invasion
	1996	CIA coup *
Korea	1894-96	Military Intervention

Appendix A

	1950-53	Military Intervention
South Korea	1950-	Occupied
Korea	1904-05	Military Intervention
Laos	1971-73	Attack
	1958	Elections sabotaged
	1962	Military Intervention
Lebanon	1982-84	Military Intervention
	1958	Military Intervention
	1982	Invasion
Liberia	1990	Military Intervention
	1997	Military Intervention
Libya	1981	Attack
	1986	Attack
	1986	Attack
	1989	Attack
Macedonia	2001	Military Intervention
Mexico	1914-18	Military Intervention
	1913	Military Intervention
Myanmar	1958	Government undermined
Nicaragua	1912-33	Military Intervention
	1981-90	Revolt, CIA inspired
	1894	Military Intervention
	1896	Military Intervention
	1898	Military Intervention
	1899	Military Intervention
	1907	Military Intervention
	1910	Military Intervention
	1981	Revolt, CIA inspired
Oman	1970	Indirect (via Iran) Invasion
Panama	1901-14	Military Intervention
	1895	Military Intervention
	1918-20	Military Intervention
	1989-90	Invasion
	1908	Military Intervention
	1912	Military Intervention
	1925	Military Intervention
	1958	Military Intervention
	1964	Military Intervention

	1989	Military Intervention
Peru	2000	CIA coup *
Philippines	1898-1939	Occupied
	1948-54	Military Intervention
	1989	Military Intervention
Puerto Rico	1898-	Military Intervention and occupied
	1950	Military Intervention
Russia	1918-22	Military Intervention
Samoa	1899-	Occupied
Somalia	1992-94	Military Intervention
Sudan	1998	Attack
Turkey	1922	Military Intervention
Uruguay	1947	Threatened Attack
Venezuela	1920	Invasion
	1962	Invasion *
	2002	CIA coup *
Vietnam	1954	Threatened Attack (nuclear)
	1961	Attack in South Vietnam (poison gas)
	1963	CIA coup in South Vietnam
	1945-54	Aided, supported, and eventually paid for French re-colonization
	1954-64	Covert action throughout Vietnam, post- French
	1964-75	"Vietnam War"
Yemen	2000	Attack
Yugoslavia	1992-94	Military Intervention
	1919	Military Intervention
	1946	Attack
	1999	Attack
Zaire	1961	Assassination
	1965	CIA coup
	1996-97	Military Intervention

www.ingramcontent.com/pod-product-compliance
Lightning Source LLC
Chambersburg PA
CBHW060302290526
45789CB00001B/380